Praise for *end your story. Begin your life...*

"*There are no fancy poses or intricate breathing techniques in here, but this is the real deal. Such a beautiful teaching. So lucid and clear. Let go of your imaginations about who you are and what the world is, your 'story,' and discover your true nature. I have known Jim for almost thirty years now. We struggled together toward clarity. He has done an excellent job of clearly stating both the practice and the teaching, making it relevant to life as we know it, and making it a fun, interesting read.*"
> —Erich Schiffmann, author of *Yoga: The Spirit and Practice of Moving into Stillness*

"*A powerful and wisdom-rich book that will help you reclaim your greatest life.*"
> —Robin Sharma, author of the national bestsellers *The Monk Who Sold His Ferrari* and *The Saint, The Surfer and The CEO*

"*I love this book! It is for anyone who is serious about enlightenment and the freedom it brings. Through his own experience and wisdom, Jim Dreaver demystifies awakening and—using the simple tools he calls the teaching and the practice—makes its realization more tangible and reachable with every page. Profound and comprehensive, easily understandable, and down-to-earth practical, this manual may literally shorten a seeker's path by decades.*"
> —Madhukar Thompson, author of *The Odyssey of Enlightenment*

"*Steeped in rich personal experience,* end your story. Begin your Life ... *makes complex and confusing Eastern concepts accessible to the Western mind. With extraordinary clarity and simplicity, this book takes us on a journey that leads to the fulfillment of our deepest hopes and longings.*"
> —John Amodeo, Ph.D., author of *The Authentic Heart* and *Love & Betrayal*, and co-author of *Being Intimate*

"*Written in a simple, straightforward style, this book is a real gift to the world. I'd call it a primer for living.*"
—Susan Campbell, Ph.D., author of *Getting Real* and *Truth in Dating*

"*This is the book all seekers of spiritual awakening have been waiting for. Jim takes the ageless spiritual truths from the East and presents them in a practical, easily understood manner from a Western perspective. Jim's book will get you onto the right path to spiritual fulfillment; it changed my life and will change yours as well.*"
—Bob Nozik, MD, Prof. Emeritus, University of California San Francisco Medical Center, author of: *Happy 4 Life: Here's How to Do It*

"*For many, life can feel like a skipping record—the same patterns repeating themselves over and over again creating a narrative that limits our ability to truly live.* end your story. Begin your life... *is overflowing with wisdom. Jim Dreaver's words are both inspiring and life-changing. This book offers a powerful, yet simple path that leads from the prison of the mind to the expanded freedom that is potential in everyone.*"
—Darren Main, author of *Yoga and the Path of the Urban Mystic*

"*To us Jim's teaching is most similar to Eckhart Tolle, but unlike Tolle, who had an unexpected spontaneous awakening, Jim's awakening came after years of spiritual seeking. His book,* end your story. Begin your life..., *makes his teaching easy to relate to and his guidance down-to-earth and helpful.*"
—Lyra Mayfield & Charlie Stein, Boulder, Colorado

"*In this book, Jim has simplified and made very clear that which cannot be spoken. His words are powerful and go right to the heart of what's true: everything between your ears is a story. I've been a seeker for over 38 years. Jim's book helped me to see that seeking is also a story. The practice of freedom itself is priceless.*"
—Stefano Siciliano, Nellysford, Virginia

end your
story.
Begin
your
life...

Mastering the Practice of Freedom

Jim Dreaver

Satori Books

Satori Books
Los Angeles, California
www.satoribooks.com

Also by Jim Dreaver:

Nonfiction:

The Way of Harmony
The Ultimate Cure
Somatic Technique (www.somatictechnique.com)

Fiction:

Falling Into Light (www.fallingintolight.com)

Library of Congress Control Number: 2009909984

ISBN 978-0-615-32423-4

For Adam, with love…
And for his generation,
And all the generations to come…

"Whoever enters the Way without
a guide will take a hundred years
to travel a two-day journey."

Rumi

Contents

Vision

I have a vision... The world is at peace, at last. It is a dynamic, vibrant, and creative peace. All the countries of the world are basically like one big, happy family. Sure, they continue to bicker and squabble with one another, as families do, and they still have their own internal problems to do with their economies, environmental challenges, and different social issues.

However, there is enough real consciousness throughout humanity to ensure cooperation and harmony between nations. There is an end to wars and terrorism. There is a more even distribution of wealth, which means extreme poverty and hunger are now rare. Very few are oppressed or down-trodden.

People throughout the world have each others' best interests at heart. They care about, support, and cheer each other on. Competition takes the form of everyone encouraging each other to be their best, and to excel at whatever they do. With so much love and goodwill in the air, peace really does prevail on earth.

So how did this happen? It is simple. Enough of us looked inwards long enough to wake up to the wisdom, love, and freedom inside us. We realized that the entire conceptual realm between our ears—all our personal, cultural, national, religious, and ethnic stories—was not fundamentally real.

We saw that the stories we tell, to ourselves and others, appear and disappear, shift and change, yet we, as the awareness or consciousness which notices them, which creates them, are ever-present, always here. We came to the realization, in other words, that there are no enemies, except those we fabricate in our own minds. This knowing frees us from psychological and emotional suffering, and is the source of our individual and collective peace, joy, and meaning.

This, then, is my vision. The book you hold in your hands is my plan for helping make it a reality. If the vision resonates with you, share it with others. Awakening to the truth of who and what we are is the most important task facing us. It always has been, only now more so than ever. Working together, we can change the world.

Introduction

T he teaching and the practice making up the heart of this
book come directly out of my own experience as a seeker
of truth. I was on a spiritual journey for twenty years, seeking
enlightenment, or inner freedom.

Then, in the spring of 1995, my seeking came to an end. I
finally realized my true nature and have been at peace, free of
conflict and suffering, ever since. The main elements of my own
story, the story of how I came to the understanding that I am
not my story, are in this book.

However, I will relate one key story now. Between September,
2003 and the end of January, 2004 I experienced a health crisis
which literally turned my life upside down. I had three strokes,
each worse than the last. The third stroke landed me in the
hospital for six days, four in intensive care. When I came out, I
couldn't move the right side of my face, my right arm and hand
were severely impaired, I walked with a limp on the right side,
and I had difficulty thinking and speaking. It took me almost
two years to recover.

Soon after the strokes, a few people who didn't know me
well said things like, "Gosh, it must have been really scary for
you," or "You must have been terrified." But the truth was I
wasn't afraid. After all, I had already realized my true nature.
I knew myself as pure consciousness, that which was not born
and does not die. When you live knowingly as the awareness you
are, fear and other negative emotions cannot touch you, other

than momentarily. You just flow with whatever is happening.

As I see it, this is the litmus test of our freedom: how we deal with life's changes and challenges. The more unconscious and unaware we are, the more such challenges will cause us to spiral down into fear, unhappiness, depression, despair, suffering, and misery. The more conscious and aware we are, the more we discern the difference between real and imaginary challenges.

From this place of clarity and present-time awareness, we deal with whatever actual challenge may be confronting us, meeting it calmly and confidently, with wisdom and love. Whether it is a relationship issue, a work problem, a financial struggle, a health crisis, a natural disaster unfolding, or a terrorist act in the making, we draw upon all the creative powers at our disposal to address it. We stay with it and respond to its call for as long we need to.

This is why I have written this book. If you absorb the teaching in these pages, and learn to do the practice every time you experience emotional conflict, upset, or suffering, you will yourself awaken to freedom, to the inner peace that does not depend on circumstances, much, much quicker than I did. As an example of how this can happen, read Juliana Dahl's story at the beginning of Chapter One. She is the mother of four children, and awakened to her true nature just three short years after we met.

The teaching itself is simple. It is to grasp that while we are a story-telling people, the stories we tell come and go, they change, but *we*, in our essence, are always here. We, as the pure awareness that sees and knows are still here, still looking through our eyes, sensing with our body, feeling with our heart and gut. Realizing we are that which is always present, and *not* the thought or story, which is ever-changing, is to be awake and free.

The practice of freedom, which is also simple, helps you embody the teaching and make it your lived experience. I will describe the practice at the end of this Introduction. The first time I discovered it was working for people was when I was teaching a workshop at the famed Esalen Institute. Esalen is an alternative education and retreat center devoted to the exploration of human potential, situated on California's rugged Big Sur coast.

On the third morning of the five-day workshop, one of the women participants came in and reported having been to Esalen many times during the past few years, and telling of a man on the staff with whom she had some personal issues. Well, she saw the man that morning and was trying to figure out a way to avoid him, when she suddenly remembered the practice I taught.

As soon as she became aware of her discomfort, she stopped and did something she had never tried before: she became very present with her experience of conflict. Then she looked inwardly at the story she was telling herself about this man: basically, "How can I avoid him?" She noticed it was just a _story_, a thought. In almost the same breath, she saw she was not the story, not any story. Rather, she was what _looked_ at the story. She was the lucid, ever-present awareness _behind_ the story.

When she saw this, a magical thing happened. As the story dissolved before her eyes, the emotional tension created by being identified with the story and wanting to avoid a confrontation also dissipated, and she felt freer, clearer, more _here_. She then went up to the man and had a totally fresh, new interaction with him.

Of course, she didn't become completely free from one moment of insight, but it was a beginning. It cracked an opening in the shell of her ego and all the stories holding it together. She experienced a glimpse, a taste, of the inner freedom which is her true nature.

Freedom is a powerful word. It is perhaps one of the most cherished words in the English language. Certainly it is so here in America, where we value our freedom more than anything. Yet what does it mean, to be free?

At the level most people relate to the notion of freedom, it means the freedom to express ourselves in whatever way we wish: to choose our work or career, our friends, our politics, our religion, to choose where we live.

Yet based on my life experience, I have a very different understanding of freedom. At its most vital level, it means the freedom to *be*, to be the beautiful, conscious person you are. It is to be *inwardly* free, not restricted or bound by any mental or emotional limitation, not subject to any emotional reactivity. Being free means feeling relaxed, at peace, and open in each and every moment. This was the experience of the woman at Esalen during her moment of awakening.

So, how do you get to this state of inner freedom, the freedom simply to *be*? The quickest path I know of, and the subject of this book, is to undergo the shift in perception which leads directly to inner freedom. It is seeing, like the woman at Esalen, that you are *not* your story. You are not any story. You are not your psychological and emotional history, nor are you your self-image. You are not your cultural, ethnic, national, social, or religious story.

And what is a story? It is anything we think or say to ourselves or others to describe what has happened, is happening, or is going to happen in the future. Some stories are true, and some are fictional, but either way they are still just *stories*, a collection of words inside our heads.

Problems arise and our freedom is hindered when the story defines us, when we derive our identity, our sense of meaning from it, as in: "*Things shouldn't be this way,*" "*That person is a bad person,*" "*I am totally alone, loved by no one,*" "*I was abandoned/abused as a child,*" or "*I fear God's judgment.*"

All your stories, memories, experiences, have shaped your personality but they are still only that: your *stories*. They may have been real once, or seemed real, but are definitely not real now. They are an illusory world existing between your ears, in the form of fleeting thoughts, beliefs, pictures, and ideas of "self," with corresponding feelings and emotions in your body.

When conflict or suffering arises, or when your buttons are pushed, it is because a person or an event, real or imagined, contradicts your view or expectation—your "story"—about the way things should be, or ought to be. The conflict is experienced as a disturbing feeling or emotion, whether of anxiety, anger, fear, or something else in your body.

However, the upsetting feelings and emotions only exist because of the stories feeding them, keeping them alive. And the stories, thoughts, and beliefs are always changing. They come and they go. However, when you are not holding onto any story in your mind, but are simply very aware and relaxed in the present, your emotional state is always one of ease, harmony, and flow. This is a very important point to understand if you are interested in finding true inner peace.

To know this, to find your identity not in stories, not in your body, mind, or personality, but in the moment-by-moment flow of *being* itself, is true freedom. Then we feel inspired to write a new, *conscious* story for ourselves, a story which works by supporting our own and others' well-being. We begin, literally, to infuse our lives, relationships, and work with this ever-new consciousness and the positive, creative stories flowing from it. As a result, our power to manifest what we truly need and want is greatly magnified, and living itself becomes a lot more fun.

So, this is an instruction manual on what may be the simplest and shortest way to the most liberating transformation we can undergo. Why do I say simplest and shortest? Because there is nothing you have to *do*, other than the practice, which is simply being very alert and noticing when you are getting caught up in a story.

While other, more traditional practices like meditation, prayer, yoga, and emotional release work can all be beneficial to body, mind, and spirit (and I have done them all myself) you don't actually have to do any of them in order to find freedom. You don't even have to do good works to get free, although you will certainly do them as freedom becomes a reality for you.

All that is required for awakening to your true nature is to undergo this shift in perception, in the way you see and experience reality. It is a shift from experiencing life from the limited point of view of "me, myself, and my story," to seeing it from your wholeness. It is awakening to the expanded view of universal consciousness itself, the consciousness which is expressing through you, right now, in your uniquely individual personality.

Many people are still confused about awakening or enlightenment. They have many "stories" about it. One of the most common misconceptions is thinking of it as some kind of salvation or magical state of being, freeing one forever from life's problems and challenges. However, this is an idealized, mountaintop view. (There was nothing "ideal" about the strokes I had, although there were certainly gifts in the experience, as you will read at the end of the last chapter).

Awakening needs to be brought down from the detached perspective of the mountaintop into the real world of the marketplace. It needs to work in the nitty-gritty of our relationships, work, and daily lives. After all, if the truth can't flourish here, where we all live, what good is it?

The world is in crisis, suffering the constant presence of terrorism, war, injustice, oppression, poverty, hunger, and disease. All this conflict exists because people's inner unease and insecurity are projected outwardly. Struggling for some sense of meaning and purpose in their lives, they identify with and cling to a particular "story"—whether cultural, religious, political, or personal—which is continually re-created by the mind.

The story, of course, is shored up by a whole set of beliefs, judgments, and assumptions. The problem is that beliefs, by their nature, are divisive. When taken to extremes, they can result in a willingness to fight, even to kill and die, for what is so fervently "believed."

More than ever, the world needs the healing which awakening brings. The key to embodying awakening is in understanding that it is very much an inner, personal journey. You must be willing to face yourself honestly, to examine closely who and what you think you are. If you're not prepared to look deeply into this "self" you have imagined yourself to be, inner freedom will continue to elude you. You'll carry on believing whatever it is you are looking for—happiness, validation, approval, success, or freedom from self-doubt—lies somewhere outside yourself.

However, something else can help accelerate your quest for self-realization: guidance. This is why I put the Rumi quote at the beginning of this book: "Whoever enters the Way without a guide will take a hundred years to travel a two-day journey."

You can awaken on your own, without a guide, but it is not so common and usually takes a long time. Clear, objective guidance from someone already awake speeds up your journey. It also ensures you receive accurate directions for beginning the process of self-inquiry, and how to go deep with it when blocks or obstacles come up—as they will.

Throughout this book, I will be your guide. I will walk with you every step of the way, and show you what you must both *do* and *know* in order to set yourself free in the shortest time possible.

I have already spoken of the *doing*. It is the practice. You must stop and pay attention to what is happening inside you whenever you are in conflict or are upset. Then you must be present with whatever you're experiencing, be it a feeling, an emotion, or an event, *without* any story. This is the key to the practice: learning to face your fears, your conflicts, your demons without a story, without judgment, resistance, or mind games.

The practice requires an openness and emotional vulnerability. It does not mean you become a doormat, and allow people to walk over you. By all means, you make changes where change is needed or desired. You retain the ability to say "No" to unwanted experiences. But inwardly, you resist nothing. Awakening is above all a state of psychological and emotional freedom. It manifests as a non-resistance to life, an all-embracing ability to flow with life's ever-changing conditions and circumstances.

But to really unlock the secret of awakening (and to understand why it persists in remaining a "secret" in the minds of those who have not yet figured it out) there is something you have to *know*. This is the teaching.

Behind every negative emotion, every form of personal angst, there is some kind of story you are telling yourself. You have to see and recognize the story as just a *story*. It may or may not have some basis in reality, but it is only one way of seeing things, and it is not who or what you *are*.

Any story you hold onto in your mind, consciously or unconsciously, gets in the way of your ability to be present, to show up fully. Freedom lies in understanding what produces the story, what maintains resistance and perpetuates conflict, fear, and suffering within you. You need to see, from the perspective of the consciousness, the wholeness which is your true nature, through the very "me" itself. You need to see through the "I," the ego, the story-*teller* who is forming the basis of your self-identity, the "person" you think you are.

The teaching is based on nondual wisdom. It is called nondual because ultimately, there is no difference between the spiritual and the material. It is all one reality. The nondual approach is also known as the direct path to awakening. It confronts the one obstacle to true inner freedom—the belief in the sense of "I" or "me" as having a real, separate existence apart from consciousness—and reveals it to be the illusion that it is.

The world between our ears, in other words, the world of "I," "me," and "mine" is not real. It is a fabrication, a story we have spent a lifetime making up and believing. By inwardly examining our thoughts, beliefs, reactions, and ideas about ourselves, we begin to realize our personal stories are always changing.

The more we see this, the more the internal drama falls away. When we are simply present with our breathing, our body sensations and feelings, and our immediate environment itself, the story lets go of *us*. We start to know ourselves *as* the pure, luminous awareness which sees and experiences reality here and now, including the stories we tell ourselves.

This knowing may be somewhat intellectual at first, but gradually it becomes embodied. More and more frequently it becomes our lived experience, and manifests as a feeling of ease, flow, and relaxed yet alert presence. As our head clears and our heart opens further, we awaken to the true beauty and meaning of life.

Having seen that everything in our mind, including all the

seeming "obstacles," is an illusion, any barriers or obstacles in the real world suddenly become very manageable. The mind is then no longer a distraction, but a powerful ally to help us deal with the problems of living. Our life purpose becomes clear and love ultimately guides us in everything we do.

The following pages will support you in making the shift toward inner freedom. Much of the content is drawn from actual dialogues I've had with countless truth seekers, both privately and in workshops, over many years. In addition, I tell many stories to clarify my meaning, as well as offering short mini-meditations in each chapter.

Woven into each chapter is the entire, seamless, nondual approach to awakening, which states that realization is a matter of seeing you are neither your story nor your thoughts. *You are the clear, ever-present consciousness which is aware of everything, including the contents of your mind.* Throughout this book I will emphasize this teaching, repeat it in many different ways, from many different angles, again and again. This is the way to have it sink into your mind and consciousness.

As you read these pages, it should become very clear as to what is involved in seeing through your own "story" and letting go of whatever beliefs, ideas, or concepts of "self" you may still be holding onto. The more you are able to simply be present and release all you inwardly hold onto (by seeing it is not real) the more you will find yourself relaxing into the awakened awareness that is your true nature.

Then your times of inner peace and freedom will occur more and more often, and the periods of conflict, stress, and suffering will be fewer and shorter in duration. Increasingly, a heartfelt sense of love and gratitude for life will be your predominant emotional reality. Then you can share the gift of awakening with others. You can share the new story you are creating for your life. In this way, our world will gradually be made whole.

Eventually, the day will come when you will pass through the final door of self-knowing. A profound and unshakable sense of ease, presence, and beauty will then be yours.

The Practice of Freedom

The essence of the practice is learning to see and experience life as it *is*, in this very moment, free of any thoughts, concepts, beliefs, or stories. You are not projecting your own ideas or values upon what is. You are not trying to make it into what you wish or want. You are not resisting it or wanting it to be different. You are just accepting it, flowing with it and, if need be, dancing with the situation at hand, be it an internal feeling or an outer circumstance.

However, most people are so heavily identified with their core stories that they really believe they *are* their stories, and when things are going well in their lives, they tend to become complacent. They usually show little interest in awakening to deeper levels of freedom. Hence the three-step practice, below. Whether it is minor suffering, like irritation, boredom, or annoyance, or major, like the death of a loved one, a health crisis, or a financial loss, we use the suffering to initiate the practice.

Personal suffering, of any degree, becomes our doorway to freedom.

Step 1: Be Present With Your Experience

Whenever upset, conflict, or struggle arises, your emotional buttons get pushed, or you find yourself challenged in some way, learn to be present with it, to allow it to be. Learn to pay attention to any disturbance in your body, in your energy field. Be with it. Don't resist it through rationalization or analysis.

Ask yourself: "What am I experiencing right now?" Then just be aware of whatever the contraction or disturbance is. Breathe, and feel it out, attune to the sensations. Eventually, you learn to welcome such reactions. After all, they are showing you where you are not yet free.

Step 2: Notice The Story

Behind every reactive emotion, whether it is stress, self-doubt, guilt, anger, envy, jealousy, loneliness, anxiety, depression, or fear there is almost always a story, belief, or thought. Notice the "story" you are telling yourself, and the meaning you are giving it, keeping the emotion alive. It may be a story from the past triggering the reaction, or a fear of something in the future. Don't go into any new story, rationalization, or analysis. Just notice.

If it helps, you can say to yourself: "Oh, I'm getting caught up in a story again."

Step 3: See The Truth

Now take a deep, slow breath, and relax. Continue to be present with the feeling or sensation. Notice how the story, thought, or bodily sensation is always changing, shifting. It comes and it goes, appears and disappears, but "you," as an aware being, are still very much here. Your thoughts are ever-changing, but you, as the background awareness, are ever-present.

Seeing this truth from the perspective of the clear, present-time awareness you are, produces a shift in your energy. The emotional contraction will unwind, and you will feel more relaxed and at ease. You will feel more truly present, more centered and grounded. Then you see everything anew, and you can deal with what's in front of you from a place of confidence and strength. You use the power of thought consciously. You are able to communicate clearly, and create what you are passionate about.

As you master this practice, you will become freer, more present, and more in the flow more of the time. You will begin to know yourself as the awareness *behind* the story, the awareness which watches your body, mind, and personality. At some level, you begin to realize that your true, fundamental nature is clear, vibrant, present-time consciousness itself.

Eventually, if you are really curious about discovering your true nature, you will take the fourth and final step to awakening, the one that will completely and, for all intents and purposes, permanently free you.

What is the fourth step? It is to question this very "me," this "I" you take yourself to be. With deep self-inquiry you will discover it is just a "story" too—the story-*teller*. The "I" telling the story is no more real than any other thought. Even though it occupies center stage in your personal life, you cannot actually find the "I" or "me" thought anywhere in your mind.

At some point, it will dawn on you that your true nature *is* the beautiful, timeless consciousness behind everything. As consciousness, you are the source of everything you experience in your life, including the "I" thought, the ego itself, and the many stories you tell. To know this, and then to embody the knowing, is to be free.

Chapter One

Step 1—Be Present With Your Experience

The first person to ask me to be her teacher was Juliana Dahl, a mother of four children, the youngest of whom was still in high school when we met. For the next year, we dialogued twice-per-month on the phone, as she lived in Boulder, Colorado, and I was in northern California. Then, in 2006, I started traveling to Boulder to teach a series of workshops in her home. Here, in her words, is her story:

"I first got a taste of enlightenment in November of 1991 while living in Saudi Arabia. During a healing session my *kundalini* energy uncoiled at the base of my spine. It shot through my crown chakra and united me with all things as *oneness*. It was definitely a unitive experience. I felt everything surrounding me as part of me and me part of it. It was very blissful, ecstatic, and because the energy shot through my sexual chakra on its way up to the crown, I also had huge waves of sexual energy running through me. It is how I would imagine making love with the divine would be. I was in a euphoric state for days, and for six months after this opening I would swoon in ecstasy when I gazed into the eyes of the person I was with whenever this occurred.

"This experience changed my life because from that moment on, anything in my life that was not in total integrity would fall away. After about a year I returned to my ordinary way of being, with suffering and hardships meeting me daily, but this *kundalini* awakening definitely put me on my spiritual journey. I wanted to discover as much as I could about regaining the feeling of unity consciousness and the freedom I had experienced.

"It was not until January of 2004 while I was presenting a workshop on female sexuality at the Sacred Sexuality, Enlightenment, and Shamanism Conference in Santa Fe that I met Jim. The subject of his talk was *Why Enlightenment Matters*. I was drawn to attend his presentation and sat right in the front row, and knew immediately I wanted him to be my teacher. I also understood for the first time that it was not necessary to wait lifetimes to wake up. He let me know it just needed a burning desire for freedom and a fundamental shift in perception, and liberation could be ours.

"During the year I studied with him, I could gradually feel the veils of illusion dropping away. Every time I experienced suffering, I would use the simple practice he taught me, the practice that is the foundation of his work. My energy would shift, and I would feel freer and more present.

"I loved the clarity and depth of his teaching style and we soon became good friends. I gathered a group of friends in Boulder to hear Jim's teaching. He returned several different times to teach in Boulder, where I hosted him. As my relationship with Jim continued over the next two years, I realized I was getting closer and closer to the freedom I wanted to live.

"During the summer of 2008, Jim was teaching a workshop at my home. That Saturday evening, he and I were driving out to dinner. On the way, he said to me: 'I'm really happy with your progress of the path of awakening, Juliana. You really do see that everything between your ears is an illusion... well, *almost* everything. You're still identified with one story.'

"I actually pulled the car over to the side of the road when he said that. I knew exactly what he was talking about. I'd been holding onto a judgment about a former room-mate. I felt she had interfered in my relationship with my then-boyfriend, so I had asked her to move out, and I hadn't forgiven her. I said to Jim: 'My God, you are right... I see now that that, too, is just a story!'

"This realization just hastened my resolve to awaken fully, and I decided I did not want to wait any longer. I could feel that I was ready to make the permanent shift. The actual moment of awakening happened the very next day, June 1st.

"What happened was that he invited me to sit in presence with him. He asked me to go deep inside and see what there was that was keeping me from being totally free. As I shut my eyes I saw several different stories which I had bought into as reality for so many years, and which had caused me many hours, days, and weeks of pain and suffering. Each one I was able to release as I knew these scenarios were not who I was.

"Then Jim asked, 'Is there anything else which is keeping you from being fully awake and free?' I closed my eyes. This time I saw pure black void. I heard the words: 'You are empty, there is nothing else ...You are *free*.'

"When I opened my eyes I knew I had fully awakened to my true nature as pure consciousness, and knew I could experience the bliss and freedom which I had only tasted 17 years ago, all the time. Studying with Jim for these three years really focused my burning desire to have freedom, and his clarity, wisdom, and strong presence—and unwavering love and support—helped launch me back into what I have always been: 'Pure awareness, expressing through this body, mind, and personality known as Juliana.'"

I spoke on the phone with Juliana recently, almost a year after she awakened. She is living in Aspen now, enjoying the timeless peace, bliss, and fun of being free, working with her sacred sexuality clients, doing massage, teaching yoga, and sharing the message of awakening with those who are open to it.

Awakening To What We Are

Our true nature cannot be expressed in words. However, consciousness, awareness, beingness, and presence are some words that come closest to defining what we are, here, right now. We always start from this moment now, from the present.

So, what can be said to be real right now is you are alive, present, and reading this book. What is real now is your existence. You are *conscious* of existing, of being alive. Your true nature *is* consciousness itself. It is the one thing always present, whether you are asleep or awake, and whether you are aware of it or not.

What you are in your essence is the lucid, unchanging consciousness giving birth to everything in the world of the senses, including all your thoughts, stories, memories, and to your body, mind, and this unique personality called "you." To understand this is to grasp the literal meaning of the words attributed to St. Francis: "What we are looking for is what is looking." You become aware of yourself, your true nature, *as* consciousness, awareness, or presence itself.

Now, most people are not aware of this. They tend to live as if in a dream—a dream which sometimes turns into a nightmare. They take their ego and their thoughts—the personal "self" and its many stories—to be real, are caught in habitual patterns of conflict, self-doubt, and worry, and have only occasional glimpses of the timeless beauty and mystery of existence.

The goal of spiritual or transformational work is to wake up from the dream. It is to break free of the internal dialogue. It is to see through the mind-created illusion of "me, myself, and my story," the imaginary world you have created between your ears, making you feel separate and apart from others.

These stories, memories, and experiences have shaped your personality but they are still only your *stories*. They may have been real once, but are definitely not real now. They are an imaginary world existing inside your head, in the form of fleeting thoughts, beliefs, pictures, and ideas of "self," with corresponding feelings and emotions in your body. And they are always changing, always coming and going, yet *you*, as the awareness which sees them, experiences them, are always here.

Every time you see the truth of this, your head clears, your body relaxes, your heart opens, and you experience a release from inner conflict, stress, and suffering. You become, in a word, *present*.

Awakening itself is realizing you are not your stories, not your thoughts, but you are the consciousness in which stories and thoughts—in which all existence—arises. You are not an object, a human being in space and time who has only intermittent glimpses of consciousness, the source of creation. You are not a wave, occasionally remembering your connection to the ocean. Rather, you are consciousness itself, viewing all of creation through the eyes of this human being called "you." You are the ocean itself, manifesting in this individual human wave form.

As this realization occurs, you find yourself connected to an inexhaustible source of wisdom, love, and inner joy. Instead of living out of some myth or story about who you are and what life means, you live in awareness in the present. Meaning and identity no longer depend on beliefs, stories, or circumstances, but flow directly out of the beauty and dynamism of the life force itself. They arise from the sense of oneness, of the intimacy you feel with life—from the fullness and fragrance of *being* itself. You live in a state of openness, of welcoming everything that comes into your awareness.

With this awakening to the truth of being, the incessant chatter of the mind no longer dominates your consciousness. Your inner state becomes one of clarity and ease—at times, radiantly so. You become aware of a deep, vast silence, a universal spaciousness without center and without borders. You feel yourself to be one with that silence.

From within this inner silence you use thinking—including the "I" thought—for the extraordinary creative tool it is, but there is no attachment to thinking itself, nor to the concepts "I," "me," and "mine."

Whenever you use these personal pronouns you are clear you are speaking as impersonal consciousness, expressing through your personal form. You use them in a functional way, free of personal ownership, pride, or emotional reactivity. Because of this openness and freedom from ego, from attachment to the personal perspective, living becomes much more effortless. Regardless of what is occurring, each day has a quality of magic and adventure to it.

Contrast this with your experience when you have not yet awakened to truth. Whenever you say "I" or "me," there is a very definite identification with the personal, with the ego self—with some kind of story, judgment, expectation, assumption, or agenda. You often feel divided, as in: "A part of me feels *this* way, and yet another part of me feels *that* way."

There may be glimpses, but there is no abiding awareness of being one with the totality of consciousness. Instead, separation, isolation, and a feeling of aloneness, even meaninglessness, is the prevailing experience. It is this personal identification with your story, with who you "think" you are, which triggers self-doubt, stress, worry, and fear. It perpetuates the experience of conflict and suffering.

Awakening, as will become clear, means freedom from conflict and suffering. This is the promise of the inner quest. It doesn't matter what your circumstances are, or where in this world you live—inner freedom can be yours, simply because it *is* your true nature.

The feeling-tone associated with being established in pure consciousness is one of relaxed ease, harmony, and presence, of openness and welcoming, of gratitude and appreciation. It is one of feeling the energy of aliveness in your body. Thoughts may or may not be present, but you are not identified with them. There is no "you" in the way. There is just the flow of beingness, what in Zen is called the "suchness" of life, and you are one with the suchness. Everything then happens out of oneness.

Truly, to know yourself as consciousness, and then to embody the knowing, is the greatest blessing…

See if you can feel it, your true nature, right now. Just be very present, very aware of all that is... Then let the awareness which you are permeate your body... Notice how your breath flows in and flows out in the awareness you are... Then notice how sensations arise and fall in your body... How thoughts, images, and stories come and go in your mind... Be aware of yourself as the awareness, the consciousness, which is aware of all this...

Getting Our Stories in Perspective

Many people have a problem, and go into resistance, when I say that they are not their story. After all, they are so identified with their story. In fact, the history of humanity is one vast interwoven story. It was the theologian, Ann Foerst, who described us as a story-telling people—*homo narrandus*. There are as many stories as there are people, and it is natural and human to share our stories with each other.

A story is simply anything we think or believe, or tell to others, to explain what has happened, is happening, or is going to happen in our lives. It is the way we derive a sense of meaning and purpose in our lives, until we tap into a deeper level of being and no longer depend on any story for our identity.

There are stories of need and desire, abundance and lack, contentment and dissatisfaction, success and failure, justice and chaos, wealth and poverty, health and disease, hope and despair. Sometimes our stories are mundane and ordinary, sometimes they are fun and even exciting, or inspiring; and sometimes they are painful or sad. Stories or parables also serve as teaching devices. We learn from them. We use them as teaching tools to illustrate certain lessons. But whatever emotion they evoke or lessons they teach us, our stories are not who or what we are. They are only *expressions* of who we are.

Those who are in the process of awakening to truth and

inner freedom understand this at some level. They learn from the story but they don't get lost in the drama of it. Instead, they derive their identity from simply being alert and present in each moment, from the flow of energy and fullness being felt right *now*.

However, most people are still identified with some kind of story at the personal, self-defining level. The attachment to these stories creates the emotional experience of either heaven or hell, or something in between the two, in our bodies, minds, and hearts. Strong emotions are always the result of being identified with a story. When we are simply present as the awareness we are, not identified with any story, our emotional state is always one of ease, harmony, and flow.

Until we go through this shift in identity and as long as we don't know ourselves at the level of pure, primordial consciousness, we are doomed to a life of uncertainty, anxiety, and suffering.

Suffering is the personal response, through the creation of a story in one's mind, to pain or unwanted experience. For suffering to arise there has to be someone—a "person," an "I," a "me"—who suffers. People always have a story around their suffering. Or, to put it another way, pain plus a story equals suffering.

However, as you become inwardly freer, pain or unwanted experience is just that—pain or unwanted experience. You may initially get upset about an event, but you remember who and what you are—pure consciousness, expressing in this body, mind, and personality called "you"—and you just deal with it. You do not create a story around it—or, if you do, it is a functional, factual story. It is a story which describes what actually happened, or is happening.

Almost all the human suffering in the world is due to the identification with a story of some kind—from people taking their stories to be reality. It may be a personal story of abandonment, loneliness, guilt, or fear. It may be a story of power and control. It may be due to a state-imposed religious story with its own harsh or restrictive edicts and subsequent denial of human rights. It may be a self-imposed religious story with a whole set of beliefs and dogmas, which you then feel compelled to embrace.

The more entrenched you are in your own story, your own version of "truth," the more you will likely resist what I am sharing. Whether it's some personal story of insecurity, pride, or fear, a cultural story causing you to be identified with a particular ethnic group or custom, or one of the many religious stories that have always been promoted as the "truth and the way" to humankind, you will tend to cling even more tightly to it. A lot of fear can come up as you contemplate the letting go of a story, any story, with which you have previously been identified.

In my work, people sometimes ask me, "But who or what am I *without* my story?" When you know the answer to that question, know it in the depths of your being, then you'll be free and your search for yourself will be over. It is my intention to guide you, the reader, gently and skillfully toward the answer, but I can tell you this right now: you will find it on virtually every page of this book.

Welcome Your Experience

A lot of people have trouble welcoming very unpleasant experiences. That is natural, yet if you are truly committed to awakening, eventually you will learn the subtle art of welcoming.

For now, it is enough to simply be present with what you are feeling or experiencing. In time, as you become freer of all that binds you, welcoming will be easier. In fact, you begin to develop an attitude of "Bring it on…!" You *want* to see where you still get caught in suffering or reaction, because you want to be free of those demons.

You have to accept, and ultimately welcome, whatever arises within your experience. After all, it is what *is*. It is reality, and as the spiritual teacher Byron Katie says, when you argue with reality, you always lose. But when you accept what is, then you are in harmony with it, and you can work to change it, heal it, or fix it.

Until awakening begins to become a reality, most people have difficulty being fully present, especially being present without an agenda. They invariably require an agenda. It may be a shared interest, a personal or business meeting with a particular focus, or some kind of gathering for a specific purpose.

In this work, you are using your own suffering as an agenda for being present. You are not denying it, you are not trying to avoid it or escape it. You are not trying to rationalize it or understand it through some form of mental analysis. You are facing it head on by accepting it, and even, as I said, welcoming it.

Now you may immediately realize the totality of the situation. You may notice the story you are telling yourself that is triggering the upset and you may grasp, even affirm to yourself, "I am *not* my story." This may produce a shift. Suddenly you are fully present, no longer caught up in any self-identifying story. You may have a glimpse of your true nature, of what you *are*. You are the consciousness which is aware.

But for many of you the shift in identity will be brief and you will revert again to getting caught up in your story. But at least now you know. You've had an "Ah ha!" moment. You've tasted the truth of your being.

Keep persisting with the practice of alert presence and I promise you it will get easier. You'll have more and more awakened or enlightened moments. The body has a cellular memory of wholeness and ease. It remembers its natural state. When you are in the state of wholeness, it's almost as if the cells are saying, "Ah, this is how I'm *supposed* to feel." Then life itself will feel smoother, more harmonious, more flowing.

The idea of welcoming as being true acceptance played a vital role in my own awakening. The more I was willing to acknowledge I *wasn't* free, I was still in conflict or suffering, the closer I found myself moving toward true freedom. And the single most powerful *mantra* precipitating my awakening and which I used whenever I was conflicted was this:

"Ah, I welcome this experience. It is showing me where I am not yet free."

In other words, you've got to befriend your upsets, shadows, demons, and negative emotions. You have to stop running from them and turn to face them. This contradicts our learned tendency, which is to live in resistance and denial. The power of adopting a truly welcoming attitude indicates your acceptance of where you are right now. You may not like it but you accept it. Acceptance, in turn, brings an immediate relaxation, an ease of being and an allowing which may then open the door for the shift in perception called awakening.

Jean Klein, the man who played the role of my spiritual guide, or teacher, and who I first met in 1984, talked about the importance of welcoming. "Welcome your experience," he used to say.

After all, openness, acceptance, and surrender to what is create a surer path to freedom than resistance and struggle. You must sink deep within yourself to find out who and what you are, and you cannot do so if you are fighting with what is or are struggling against your situation in any way.

Born in Europe, Jean studied music in Vienna, fought in the French resistance during the Second World War, and became a naturopathic physician. But he always had a passionate interest in truth, in a way of living free of the materialistic addiction sweeping Europe after the war. As a result, he spent a number of years in India studying with several spiritual masters.

In time, he became a master in his own right, a skilled exponent of Advaita Vedanta. This is the enlightenment tradition known as the "direct path" or the nondual path because it points directly to consciousness, to the one energy which is our true nature.

Jean was an urbane, cultured, and intellectually sophisticated man. Even though he was in some ways detached from the normal hurly-burly of the marketplace and had more of a mountaintop teacher's style about him, he was still in the world. He wasn't a white-robed, celibate, ascetic teacher completely withdrawn from everyday life. He enjoyed the finer things in life. While he could sometimes be aloof, he remained one of us, and he always emphasized the simple but profound truth of awakening: the terms "teacher" and "student" are only a device. When you realize you are, in your essence, the same, beautiful person you took your teacher to be, you will be free.

Soon after I met him, I had a private session with him. With all the eagerness of a true seeker, I told him that I felt I needed to divorce my wife, who didn't support my spiritual practice, leave my son, close my chiropractic practice, and go live in a retreat somewhere where I could meditate for long hours every day, and really focus my energy on the quest for enlightenment.

He looked at me for a few moments, his clear blue eyes sparkling and twinkling. (He probably thought to himself, "What on earth is this poor man thinking!") Then he smiled, and said, in his thick European accent: "Don't change anything in your life. Just be who you are. You are beautiful as you are."

Instantly, I relaxed. Later, I realized I had received a transmission, an infusion of energy from the light and warmth in his eyes. Nobody had ever told me I was beautiful as I was. I always thought I wasn't good enough. That was the moment when I began to accept myself, warts and all.

Another contribution Jean made to my understanding was the practice of stepping back with my awareness and experiencing myself as the *space* in which my body appears, in which breathing happens, in which the personality, with its sensations, feelings, and thoughts arise.

Doing this practice whenever I was anxious or stressed gave me a sense of detached presence. By "detached presence" I mean I would still feel the upsetting emotion, and yet I would at the same time have a sense of freedom from it, and the glimmerings of the realization that my true nature *was* this freedom, this spacious awareness, and *not* the emotion, or the story which was fueling it.

The focus on awakening to freedom is integral to the whole nondual approach. Become established in the openness of your true nature and then live your understanding every day. Continue with the life-long work of becoming a more compassionate and loving human being. But if you have a story about awakening as being a living exemplar of selfless love—as many people are wont to do—then you are unlikely to ever get there. You will forever fall short of your own unrealistic standards.

Awakening is waiting for every single one of us precisely because it *is* our true, inner nature. Being awake doesn't make you better or smarter than anyone else. It doesn't make you superior. All it does is set you free. It frees you from conflict, worry, and fear, and brings you back to the deep inner peace and fulfillment, the innocence and openness of mind and heart, that you once knew when you were very, very young. Except now you have the wisdom, maturity, and life experience of adulthood to serve as a protective container for this new way of seeing and being in the world.

The more of us who find the inner peace which comes with awakening to who and what we are underneath all our beliefs, myths, and stories, the more we will see peace in our world. Then our children can grow up in an atmosphere of love and caring, rather than fear and uncertainty. Then we can come together as a global community to solve the many social and economic problems facing us.

What better or more selfless motive for awakening, for enlightenment, could there be than this?

No Resistance, No Suffering

You have to be particularly alert when your story is active or when the "I" thought is occupying center stage in your consciousness. The quality of witnessing presence may be enough to stop the thoughts in their tracks.

You will begin seeing the "I" thought is not who you are. After all, you can observe the "I" thought, you can witness the machinations of your own mind. You can watch the story you tell yourself, watch it unfold. Therefore, you can't *be* the story.

You can't be the "I." You are whatever is watching. You are whatever is looking, witnessing. This is the teaching in action, seeing you are *not* your story. This in itself can bring the moment of realization.

Awakening is coming to the same realization the Buddha did: there is no independent "self." This psychological and emotional "entity" we take ourselves to be doesn't actually exist, except as an idea, a story, a fictional creation between our ears.

Due to our conditioning, the cultural and social myths we were raised with, we grow up convinced there is, indeed, a separate, special "us" living inside these bodies of ours. There is a "me" inside this body that came from somewhere prior to birth, and that will go somewhere after death. We believe this so firmly that this "me," this ego, actually feels real. The idea of letting go of it feels scary, indeed. When loneliness, depression, or unhappiness in any form strikes us, "we" certainly feel it—which just reinforces the idea there is "someone" inside this body/mind suffering.

Awakening reveals the suffering only happens precisely because we are so *identified* with our body, mind, and senses. We identify with our ego, with the concept of "me," and with all the stories that shore it up.

When we see that this "me" we have taken ourselves to be is just an idea we have been buying into, a story we have been telling ourselves repeatedly all these years, all thoughts about being a unique, separate, special "someone" dissolve, and suffering drops away. There is literally no "person" to suffer.

We return to our natural state, to our true identity as pure consciousness. We are no longer holding onto any image of ourselves or of the way things should be, so there is nothing in us to resist the flow of life.

The teaching and the practice are the tools you will use whenever you find yourself in a state of conflict, upset, worry, or suffering. They will help you get clear. They will enable you to move your energy quickly and efficiently whenever you feel uncomfortable, stressed, or anxious. They will empower you to shift your state of consciousness from one of contraction into one of expansion and ease.

Eventually, as you work with the teaching and the practice, they will become one. They will become second nature, like breathing, moving, sensing, and feeling. When the teaching and the practice become one you will find yourself at the doorway to true inner freedom. You may not be completely free, but you will realize you are free enough, and that most of your worry and fear stories have left you. The inner dialogue will wind itself down and you will simply be more present. You will now be a person pretty much at peace with yourself.

Self-doubt, personal conflict, and suffering will rarely visit you anymore. When they do, you will quickly notice yourself getting caught up in conflict, in some story you are telling yourself. Then you do the practice. Use the welcoming *mantra*: "Ah, I welcome this situation. It is showing me where I am not yet free." Notice the story, and the very noticing will be your key to come back to a heightened awareness, to alertness and openness in the present moment.

To Be Present Is To Live In The Now

How do you know when you are present? When there are no stories or thoughts distracting you, so that your mind is clear and your attention is fully, alertly here—here right now—then you are present. Your body feels relaxed. You're like a perfectly spinning top, humming in place without the slightest wobble, but with a consciousness very attuned to what is going on within and around you. You're totally in the flow of the moment, awake and sensitive to all that is...

Be like that top now. Try stepping back behind
yourself with your awareness... Step back out
of the story, away from the contents of your
mind... Then visualize yourself as empty space

*on the inside... Vast, empty space, yet containing
whole worlds, including the world of your body,
mind, and personality, as well as all thoughts,
your stories... You are this very clear awareness,
simply present with it all... Get the sense of
being this... This humming presence, this all-
knowing consciousness... Then open your eyes,
and be the awareness which you are...*

I remember taking a hike in the hills above Santa Rosa one day, many years ago, with my friend, Erich Schiffmann, a yoga master, from whom I first heard the spinning top analogy. We were talking about yoga and other approaches to transformation, and what the real goal was when a teacher worked with students.

He said, "I think whatever gets them into the now moment is what it's about."

Erich's words were right on. They were a pithy yet potent Zen—or in his case—yogic teaching. The path of awakening is all about being in the now moment. It is about discovering that only the now exists, that time is an arbitrary mental construct. While functional time is the natural evolution and expansion of creation, it is still arbitrary. After all, we devised the clock. We made the decision to divide a day into twenty-four hours, an hour into sixty minutes, and so on.

Then there is psychological time, the ego, the "me" living in its story, in its memories of the past and its thoughts about the future. The "me" struggles to be present but it is haunted by the past and either lives in fear of the future, or clings to the hope of the future providing the happiness and fulfillment lacking in the now. Underneath hope, lurking somewhere deep within the psyche, is the fear of the future perhaps not turning out well after all.

People often ask me, "But what about making plans?" Planning is a function of the mind, and when you need to make plans, you make plans. But then when you have finished planning, you always come back to being aware in the present.

So long as we take ourselves to be a separate psychological/ emotional entity, so long as we remain identified with and attached to this world between our ears called "me, myself, and my story," we live in constant insecurity. Underneath all insecurity is fear. We are afraid of unwanted outcomes, of being alone, of becoming sick and helpless, and ultimately, of dying. The fear of death is not even so much a fear of the body dying, but of what happens to "me"—the person I think I am inside my body—when the body dies.

In Advaita Vedanta, this identification with "self" and "story" is called *avidya*, or ignorance. Ignorance is the fundamental error, the first mistake, the original sin. It is the equivalent of the Biblical story of the fall from grace, where Adam and Eve ate of the fruit of the tree of knowledge of good and evil— "knowledge" being a metaphor for "self" knowledge. When Adam and Eve started identifying with their personal sense of "self" and judging themselves, all their troubles began.

In the same way, we, through ignorance of our essential nature, are the creators of our own insecurity, fear, and suffering. For example, most people are afraid of death, and of what happens to *them*, the "me," when they die.

None of us can know for sure, but we can get a clear, intuitive sense of what happens. However, in order to do so, you must first find out who this person you take yourself to be is. It means asking one of the most profound and liberating questions you can ever ask yourself:

"If I can observe a thought, even the 'I' or 'me' thought, then I cannot be the thought. Who or what is observing, then? Who or what am I?"

In time, if it is not becoming clear to you already, you will realize the inner voice asking these questions is itself another thought, another concept. You will realize who and what you are is the awareness that notices and witnesses everything, including the arising of the "I" thought.

In other words, your true fundamental nature is pure, silent awareness, expressing itself through this body/mind/self called "you."

To realize your true nature is to step through the door marked "Enlightenment." It is to liberate yourself from the thought-based world inside your head. It is to discover there is only the present, this moment now. The past is a memory, and the future is simply the present expanding. And the key to discovering this is awareness or presence itself. Being supremely present and open to all of existence brings you fully into this moment, where all of creation is happening. Everything is taking place right here, right now. This moment now is reality.

Understanding this is the secret of time management. People who worry about time, who feel stressed because they feel they are running out of time, tend to live in their heads. Most of their thoughts are about the future, and how they have so much to do, and so little time.

But when you see you are not your story, not your thoughts, but are the awareness behind them, then you live in the present, in the timeless zone, as I call it. Then you have an abundance of time. No matter what your watch or the clock says, the time is always *now*. You come to realize every moment is new. It is very liberating.

A seeker once asked this question of me: "I remember when I was in high school I had a job working in a salad factory where it was freezing. It was a windowless room with fluorescent lighting. It felt like a true hell to me. The only thing keeping me going was watching the clock and wishing my day away, knowing at 4:30 I could get out of there. Isn't it only natural to hate such an environment and be glad when you can get out of it? How can you be focused on the now when you are trying to cope with a horrible now, and daydreams and fantasy are able to take you away from it?"

It is natural to dislike where we are presently when we are not yet free. This is the unawakened human conditioning, and it is called "suffering." The problem is not the now. It is this "I," this "me," this "person" you take yourself to be who is unhappy, who fondly remembers the good old days, can't stand what's currently happening, and watches the clock, or the calendar, and dreams of a better time in the future.

Enlightenment is seeing the "self" concept you have been building since about age two inside your head is totally unreal. Once you see this, once you get it, you will be awake. You will live fully and effortlessly in the present, because you will understand that the present is all that exists. You will always be at peace. You will always flow cheerfully with whatever is happening. Sure, there may be more fun awaiting you tomorrow evening, when you have a hot date or some other exciting activity planned, but you don't dwell on that.

After all, there is only now, there is only ever the now, and even working in a freezing, windowless salad factory is okay when you are inwardly free. As I advised the questioner, you may certainly form a plan, from a place of clarity and presence, to move on from the salad factory as soon as you realistically can—and, in the meantime, maybe wear an extra sweater!

Whenever you find yourself doing something you don't really want to do, it helps if you ask yourself, "If I were an enlightened Zen master (or Sufi, or Christian mystic, or whatever inspires you) how would I approach this?" Then act accordingly.

Remember, awakened people are not defined by their personal history, or any other story about reality. If they are defined by anything at all, it is the timeless beauty, vibrancy, and creative energy of this moment *now*. They honor the past, they keep an eye on the future, but they are always right here, fully appreciating and flowing with whatever is happening now.

I often get asked some version of this question: "How can I remember to be present, to be here now? It seems like I forget so easily, and then I find myself being stressed out."

This is why we do the practice. Whenever you are upset or suffering, the first thing to do is to be present with it. Then look for the story you're telling yourself, and notice you are not the story. You are the awareness *looking* at the story. Then just be present with the feeling or emotion without trying to change it, without going into your head and creating a new "story" around it.

But short of living with your own personal guru or having

a partner who is highly aware and will remind you on a regular basis (which many people would probably find, at first, very annoying!) it is inattention itself that brings you back to attention. J. Krishnamurti was the first teacher I actually heard use the phrase about the awareness of inattention bringing us back to attention.

What I have since found is it works this way: you hear the truth about being present often enough, and you begin to associate presence with the clarity, ease, and deep well-being characteristic of the awakened state. Then it becomes easy. Suffering becomes the trigger.

Whenever you feel yourself suffering, unhappy, caught in conflict, or worrying in some way, it is your reminder to breathe, be present with whatever is happening, and look for the story running you and causing your upset. Then realize you are *not* your story; you are the awareness that is here right now. So come back to being very aware in this moment now.

A person I was working with said to me once: "When I am present, there is no problem."

Interestingly, we are often the most present when facing danger or are experiencing an actual crisis. The situation demands our presence. This is why people seek out adventurous activities like mountain or rock climbing, or certain sports like surfing or snowboarding. These activities force them to be present in such a way as to make them feel really alive.

But if you take the path of awakening, you'll always feel alive, present, and engaged by the moment, no matter what you are doing. And you can still climb mountains, surf, or snowboard.

Now, what about when the emotional contraction—anger, or say fear—happens so quickly it just overtakes you, and there isn't any obvious story? When this happens, simply experience the emotion. Feel angry, feel the fear. You breathe and somehow get through it. It is important to not go into your head about it, not to try to figure out why you feel the way you do. Don't create a new story around it. When the emotion subsides, then you can go into your head and look for the story which triggered your reaction. You may have to look deeply into your past to find it.

But know this: there's *always* a story behind your anger or your fear, telling you the ways you were wronged, or how you got scared.

Meditation

Just as enlightenment is a fancy word for knowing who you are and being inwardly free, so meditation is a fancy word for being very present and watching the thoughts, sensations, and feelings arise and subside without getting caught up in them.

In the Introduction, I said you don't actually need to meditate or do anything else in particular to find the freedom of enlightenment. It is totally the result of a shift in perception, through realizing you are not your ever-changing story, not this "I" or "me" you have taken yourself to be, but that you are pure, ever-present awareness itself. There are people who have never formally meditated, yet have experienced this sudden awakening to the truth of their being, and their lives have been transformed by it.

However, if you're not yet fully awake, if you are still identified with some story or notion of "self," meditation can be a useful practice to help you quiet the mind and begin to take a closer look at this "person" you imagine yourself to be. It certainly was a vital practice for me.

The essence of meditation is to sit and just be very aware of everything going on within and around you. You can meditate for a formal period of five minutes, fifteen minutes, or an hour or longer. Meditation helps train your mind, so that you become the master of it rather than having your thoughts—the stories inside your head—control you. It helps you develop the witnessing consciousness or presence. It enables you to become the supreme watcher of your mind, emotions, and body processes. This is a very important step.

When you can slip easily into the role of the detached observer of your own internal processes, you are close to freedom. I say "close" because as long as you are still identified with some concept or image of yourself as the "witness" or "observer," you are caught in duality—"me" and "other"—and are not yet truly free. True freedom exists when you are not identified with any image or concept in your mind and are just fully aware, present, and responsive in each unfolding moment.

When you meditate, you may sit with your eyes open, or they may be closed. There are really no rules. The main thing is the quality of awareness you cultivate. When you are truly present, it doesn't matter whether your eyes are open or closed. The experience of timelessness and of alert beingness is the same.

If you take the time to sit and meditate for a while in the morning you will find it a lovely way to start the day. Of course, it won't always be so lovely in the beginning stages! Sometimes you will struggle with tension, anxiety, or other uncomfortable states. But part of meditation is dealing with all of it.

In order to be free, you must be willing to slow down and face, welcome, everything which comes up. You must be a spiritual warrior. But as you become freer, you live and move *from* freedom, and then you can move and act quickly if the situation demands it.

When you sit to meditate, or when you are driving in your car on the freeway, if you just step back with your awareness and watch your mind, your thoughts will eventually settle. Of course, while you are being aware of your mind as you drive on the freeway, you are simultaneously remaining aware of the freeway and the traffic! If you are new to meditation, getting some detachment from your mind can be difficult at first. But it will come with practice. I give a specific practice for this at the end of this chapter.

The more detachment you develop, the clearer, calmer, and more spacious your mind will feel. Then you will be able to tap into even deeper layers of consciousness. When the surface noise dies down the deeper sounds can be heard.

Albert Einstein supposedly said we use only five or ten

percent of our brain power. That's because we get caught up in the same old patterns of thought. Deepak Chopra once said we have something like 65,000 thoughts a day, and ninety percent of them are the same as the thoughts we had yesterday. Certainly not very original or creative thinking!

As space opens up in your mind, new thinking can come in. That means insight, imagination, creativity, wisdom, and even psychic abilities, such as the ability to see the future or to tune in to levels of reality not obvious to the ordinary senses. The mind itself is nonlocal, which means you can't really find it anywhere in particular. Analytical thinking, however, does have a locus or point of origination. It comes from in back of the forehead, just behind the point between the eyes known as the "third eye."

A noisy, over-active mind is one of the main barriers to freedom. Meditation is about learning to dwell in present-time awareness and to *use* thinking as a tool, rather than living out of your head, your thoughts, with only occasional glimpses of clear awareness. Then your mind no longer controls you, but rather you, as consciousness, control it.

The more you embody the quality of relaxed yet alert presence, the more you come to the place where your mind is consistently quiet, clear, and spacious. This spaciousness allows thoughts to come and go. They are no longer a problem. You no longer allow yourself to identify with them or get caught up in them. You are then able to focus your intention in a powerful way when needed, and to use your rational and intuitive modes of thinking with creativity and ingenuity.

"Do you still meditate?" is a question I am asked frequently.

When I was on the path to discovering my true nature meditation was an important daily practice for me. Initially, meditation helped me tame my wild mind, and then to dip deeper into the clarity I eventually began to experience. But once you know who and what you are, in a very real way you are always meditating. You are always aware and always present, so there is no need to formally meditate anymore. However, I still like to sit occasionally, especially in the mornings. It is good just to sit and *be*—to be quiet, alert, and very aware of all that is. It is a good time to review your intentions, what you want to manifest in your life.

D. T. Suzuki, the famous Zen master, said: "Even after enlightenment, practice must continue so as to deepen and expand the experience."

In Zen meditation the basic practice is *za-zen*, which in essence is just sitting and being present. The more you practice being consciously aware in this way, the more you embody the consciousness which you are and the more you express your true, enlightened nature in every word, action, and deed.

Let's experience true meditation, a meditation on pure being, right now...

> *Simply be present with what* is... *Now take a deep, slow breath, and relax... Notice the thoughts, beliefs, or stories passing through your mind, like "I'm uncomfortable," or "This moment isn't it, there has to be something more..." Then observe how everything that can be seen appears and disappears, including these thoughts, but you, as pure awareness, are always here... Every thought, sensation, and feeling shifts and changes... But* you *are the ever-present awareness behind everything... So feel the energy of your true nature... Be the awareness you are...*

Use Your Meditation As A Tool For Exploration

Someone once said to me: "I had many questions I wanted to ask my teachers, both in school and college, as well as spiritual teachers I have sat with. But most of the time I have been too nervous, too afraid to speak up, or when I finally did summon up the courage, it was too late, and I missed my opportunity. How can I deal with this—even better, be done with it once and for all?"

I advised this person this way: "When looking for the story you are telling yourself, you may have to ask: 'So, what is it about the nervousness I feel whenever I go to ask a question? Where does it come from? What is the fear about?'"

This is self-inquiry in action. You have to bring real awareness, presence to the inquiry. In fact, your presence is the most powerful transforming agent available to you. When you practice the power of presence throughout the day, day in and day out, eventually it becomes second nature. Bring this presence into your meditation, face your fears—those painful memories from the past—in this alert, open way and they begin to lose their power over you.

More and more you realize that what you actually are *is* the clear, present-time awareness, or consciousness, which looks at the story or at the memory. Then the memories and stories lose their emotional charge. They cease being a button or trigger for you. No one can push that button any more, or at least in any significant way.

You are human, and there will still be residues. You may still have a tendency to get nervous when asking a question, but you will just get very present, breathe, be totally in the moment, and you'll put up your hand and ask the question anyway. Maybe there will be a slight catch, a hint of nervousness in your voice, but it won't matter. It's no big deal. It won't stop you. You will no longer be blocked by the fear.

Many of our past memories are unconscious so they may not surface right away. You may not see the story immediately. So, you simply live with the question. Every day when you sit to meditate, you bring it up and look at it anew. You keep it at the back of your mind during the day.

So long as you define the question clearly—"What is going on with me in this particular instance? Why am I being triggered so?"—I assure you, the answer will eventually come, and usually it will come sooner rather than later. We always get what we ask for. It is a law of the universe.

Perhaps it will come in a dream, when you are washing your hair in the shower, or when you are getting a massage or bodywork. It can even happen when you are making love. When you live with the question, you can be doing anything, and then suddenly, at the most unexpected moment, the forgotten memory or image will pop into your mind. Once you have seen it, you won't forget it.

Then, as soon as you get some alone time, sit down in meditation, or take a meditative walk out in nature, and face it. Shine the light of awareness on the memory, the story, the button that was pushed.

Remember, this work of self-inquiry is not about denying or rejecting your feelings and emotions. But you must understand that the unresolved memories, especially the memories associated with shame, betrayal, abandonment, rejection, or failure, keep the negative feelings alive. These negative feelings are experienced as guilt, envy, jealousy, resentment, loneliness, depression, meaninglessness, and despair. All of these feelings have some kind of a story behind them. The story is what fuels them.

So, when the feelings and emotions arise, be present with them, even welcome them from the perspective of them showing you where you are not yet free. Then look at the story you are telling yourself. The story is what keeps the negative feelings and emotions alive. The more you let go of the past, the story, the freer you are of those feelings. And you let go of the story by seeing that it isn't real.

But as you let go of the story, if you feel you are having difficulty with the disturbing emotion, then face the upset directly. Locate it in your body. Be very present with it. Don't try to analyze or understand it. Don't go into your head. Don't create more story around it. Just be very alert and watch it. If you don't interfere with the story-making mind, with the "I" or "me," the energy will soon shift. You will feel more relaxed, whole, and present.

The great teaching of Advaita, the nondual path, is that

these stories and memories have no reality in the present. They are illusions that appear real when we cling to them, when we identify with them. This must be seen again and again. You must bring a powerful presence to the seeing so that it comes alive, is dynamic.

When you actually see this, your mind clears, your emotions become stable and harmonious, and you feel good inside. You feel relaxed and at ease in the present. Then your emotional energy flows much more spontaneously and authentically. You may cry when something sad happens; you may get angry when you see injustice being perpetrated; you may laugh when you hear something funny. But it all happens naturally, and there is no holding onto anything. You are just here in the present, dancing with the ever-changing, ever-new, ever-interesting drama of creation.

In a very real way, it is like being a child again. Young children live very much in the moment. They feel things deeply and then they let them go as their eyes open with fresh wonder at something new happening. To be free is having this child-like quality of innocence and newness, except that you also have all the wisdom from decades of living.

Suzuki-roshi, the Zen master who inspired so many Americans to take up Zen, called it beginner's mind. He said: "In the beginner's mind there are many possibilities, but in the expert's, few."

Dive Into The Well Of Your Own Being

There are many physical practices and disciplines available to help you awaken to the energy of your true nature.

Yoga is one such practice. I discovered it in my late twenties, and it taught me to be supremely present in my body, and supremely present with my awareness. And even though the health benefits of doing yoga, such as stretching and relaxing muscles, increasing flexibility, and enhancing health and vitality are significant, there is another, more vital benefit, as well.

Patanjali, the ancient philosopher of yoga, in the opening verses of his *Yoga Sutras*, stated: "Yoga is the stilling of the thought waves of the mind."

When the thought waves of the mind become calm and still, there is no longer any disturbance, conflict, or fear present in the psyche. Then we can see reality with startling clarity, and we feel connected to the awesome power and energy behind creation itself—the energy of our true nature.

Yoga brings about an integration of body, mind, and spirit. Doing the yoga postures, or *asanas*, is a moving meditation. The pauses and periods of stillness in between them can be profoundly blissful and healing. Whenever you bring a heightened awareness to your body, inhabiting your body more consciously, you feel its aliveness more acutely. Tuning in to sensation and feeling at a somatic level takes you out of your mind. Releasing the problems associated with thinking gives you a direct experience of the fullness and power of *now*. Bringing a heightened consciousness to your body is one of the keys to awakening.

I first discovered this when I was studying yoga with Erich Schiffmann. Not long after our friendship began, I was hanging out with him one weekend afternoon at his house. We did some yoga together, and then decided to sit in meditation. As we closed our eyes and sat, I noted the usual tension in my body, and the restless noise and chatter in my mind. The longer I sat, and the more I slowed my breathing, the more my mind quieted down.

Yet the real peace and serenity, which I had tasted in brief moments of yoga and meditation, eluded me. I had only been on my spiritual path a few years. The whole journey of awakening was still fairly new to me. I was grateful to have Erich as a friend, a fellow-traveler, and a guide on the path.

After sitting for perhaps fifteen or twenty minutes, I started to get restless again. I opened my eyes to sneak a look at Erich. His eyes were closed, and he had a peaceful smile on his face. Whatever his inner experience was, it obviously felt good to him. Clearly, he was deeply connected to some source of inner joy, and the realization caused a pang of envy within me. I almost wanted to say to him, "Hey, what have you found in there? I want some, too."

Then I heard myself saying, "Well, Jim, why don't you go within? Why don't you dive inside yourself, and see if you can find the same place within you?"

And I did. I closed my eyes again, breathed slowly and consciously. I got very present, and let my awareness drop deep into my body. As I allowed every muscle, every single cell of my body to relax and open up, I began to feel the most exquisite energy start to move and to bubble up inside me.

It was as if every cell was being quickened, as if each cell was being gently massaged from within. It felt very blissful. As I continued to breathe consciously and allowed myself to surrender more deeply to the feeling inside me, I began to smile myself. In fact, it felt like my whole being was smiling on the inside.

Some time later, I opened my eyes, and—as these things would have it—Erich opened his at precisely the same time. We looked at each other in a knowing way, both of us smiling, and then we threw our heads back and laughed out loud. Then I put my hands together, and bowed my head, saying *"Namaste,"* a Sanskrit word which means, "I honor the God in you… The same God that is in me." Silently, I thanked my friend for his transmission.

That was one of the most important lessons I received. By getting still and going inside, you literally dive into the well of your own being, and in this way discover the source of true well-being. You discover the healing energy of bliss—what the yogis call the *shakti* energy, the divine vibration, or feeling— that lives within us. To connect with that bliss for even a few minutes is very healing. It allows you to move through the rest of the day with clarity, ease, and presence.

A Meditation Practice

The more you practice being present, the more presence becomes second nature for you. By consciously meditating—slowing down your breathing, relaxing and sensing your body, and being fully alert and awake in the here-and-now—you begin to free yourself from the stories, thoughts, and images generating conflict, worry, and self-doubt.

(Note: In the following meditation practice you close your eyes for a period of time. Either read it through first to make sure you understand it, or have a friend read it for you and guide you through it; then you can do the same for them).

Sit in a comfortable position. Have your torso completely upright, with your lumbar spine slightly swayed, your shoulders back, your chest wide, and your head balanced perfectly on your shoulders. Let your eyes remain open, your shoulders and jaw relaxed.

Take in your surroundings for a moment or two, and then close your eyes. Breathe slowly and consciously down into your belly, pelvis, and legs. Internally visualize your breath moving downward in this way, so you feel at ease with where you are sitting.

Now let your awareness expand until it feels as if you, as a localized field of awareness, are slightly behind and above your head. From this vantage point, scan the length and breadth of your body. Make your body an object of observation, just as you would a tree, a house, a car, or a person. Get the sense of yourself, your real being, as the awareness in which your body lives. You have a body, but you are not fundamentally your body. Rather, your body is an expression, or extension of the awareness you are.

Notice your breath rising and falling within this awareness. Pay attention to the sensations and feelings shifting and changing inside your body. Notice that you the awareness observing the breath, sensations, and the feelings. Now pay attention to the stories, thoughts, ideas, and images passing through your mind. Notice how you have them too, but they are not who you really are. Thoughts, even judgmental or negative thoughts, simply come and go within the larger field of the awareness you are...

Notice how you can make thought an object of observation in the same way you can observe your body, your breath, or anything else. Watch your thoughts as if they were birds flying across the sky of your mind. In simply observing them and not getting caught up in any particular thought, stillness and peace unfold.

Now let your hearing expand, and notice the sounds in your environment, whether of a bird, a car, a person's voice, or the hum of an appliance. Notice how sounds come out of silent awareness, and dissolve back into it. Notice how spacious it feels to be in this place of expanded awareness.

Gently open your eyes again. Notice how you are this very aware being, looking out through your two eyes as you feel the physicality of this body that is the vehicle, or instrument of the awareness you are. Breathe into the awareness you are...

Then slowly, consciously, rise from your chair or meditation cushion and proceed with your day.

Chapter Two

Step 2—Notice The Story

Until about the age of two, you were pure consciousness, shining through this little toddler's body known as "you." You were very aware of sensation and feeling, of sensory stimulation, but the idea of being a "self" with a personal history was unknown to you. You lived in the present. Only your experience of now was real for you.

However, somewhere about age two, the thinking faculty developed enough to discriminate between "self" and "other." You gradually began to perceive a difference between yourself and other people. You began to believe there was a unique "person" living inside you; this idea was reinforced by your family, not to mention the whole social and cultural milieu.

Thus began the fall from grace. You ate from the tree of "self" knowledge, and entered the world of duality, of "black" and "white," of "good" and "evil." You became identified with ideas of "right" and "wrong," of "good" and "bad." You began to take yourself to be a separate "person," a person who found joy in many activities and experiences, but who also went through a lot of conflict and suffering whenever things didn't go the way you wanted.

Now, as an adult, you are firmly entrenched in the belief that a distinct "you" lives inside your body that is separate from everybody else. You have forgotten your true, original nature: the ocean of pure consciousness, manifesting in the unique wave form of your particular body/mind/personality. You have made your happiness dependent on events outside yourself. You live in the past or the future, rarely in the now. The conditions of your life, to a greater or lesser degree, control you. You are emotionally reactive. Your buttons can easily be pushed.

At times, you feel like a victim of the circumstances in your life. A victim can be defined as someone who is totally identified with and at the effect of his or her story. For example, most victims are eager to tell their tale of woe to anyone who will listen. People who are caught in the trap of victim-hood are completely out of touch with their true nature.

In its simplest definition, enlightenment or awakening is rediscovering the truth of who and what you are. It is turning your gaze back in upon yourself, and waking up to the fact that the "person" you have been taking yourself to be since about age two, is in fact an illusion. It is not real.

All the beliefs, judgments, memories, opinions, labels, and experiences you have accumulated in your mind, and which make up the "story" of your life, and support the idea of being a "person" with a history, are just that—a story. The story has deep roots and has molded and shaped your personality. It has contributed to the face you now display toward the world. But in actuality, your psychological and emotional history has little to do with the reality of now, with what is actually happening right now.

All your thoughts and beliefs about who and what you are keep you from being open and available in the present. The agendas and considerations you hold inside your head, and which generate emotional tension in your body, act as a barrier between yourself and other people. They block you from truly connecting with others. They prevent the possibility of true intimacy. Ultimately, they stop the flow of love.

Whenever you find yourself in the presence of authentic love, the negative beliefs about yourself will be triggered, your buttons will be pushed, and you will tell yourself you are unworthy or undeserving. Or, you may tell yourself you *are* deserving, but then think you have to play certain games, or act in a particular way, in order to keep the love alive.

Whether it is love or just life, as long as you take yourself to be a person with a history, you are not really present. So long as you live with an image or story about "self," there will always be a problem with "self" esteem. There will always be some agenda, some consideration in your mind. You are always second-guessing yourself. You are often judging yourself, and by extension, judging others.

To be awake is to know who and what you truly are at the deepest level of your being, beyond all your thoughts, beliefs, concepts, and stories *about* who you are. It is to know and feel yourself as being one with, and an expression of, universal consciousness, manifesting in this body/mind/self called "you."

This knowing brings a tremendous sense of inner freedom, a freedom from personal conflict and suffering. It brings the experience of true inner peace, the peace which passes all understanding. Once you have awakened to that peace, once you know yourself as nothing—no "thing"—and everything at the same time, you can then share your knowing with the world. You can share your peace with the world.

Envision yourself at peace, and the world at peace. That alone should be all the motivation you need to discover the truth of who and what you are. Interestingly, I had someone say to me once: "The world at peace... Wouldn't that be kind of boring?" I responded with: "If you were truly at peace, you wouldn't ask such a question."

After all, boredom is itself a state of mind that is restless, weary, seeking some form of stimulation or excitement. True inner peace is a mind that is clear, calm, and spacious. It is a mind that is awake and alert in the present. It is a mind that is loving and fearless. It is a mind free of any thought of "self," and thus interested in and open to all possibilities.

Residues

A man once asked Jean Klein: "What if everybody in the world became enlightened?" Jean looked at the man, and then smiled. "Why," he said, "Then there would only be dancing…!"

By dancing, he meant, of course, celebration, play, and creativity. But it doesn't mean the normal human problems and challenges go away. With awakening, we don't just then abide in some kind of effortless perfection.

As Jean said on another occasion, enlightenment doesn't mean problems go away, it just means they are no longer problematic. You just deal with the challenges before you. You deal with them from a very clear, present, and responsive place.

Nisargadatta Maharaj, a guru from Mumbai, was visited by many seekers from the West. Once, one of them asked him if he still had any fears. He replied: "Occasionally an old reaction, emotional or mental, happens in the mind, but it is at once noticed and discarded. After all, one still has a personality, so one is still exposed to its idiosyncrasies and habits."

When I read this statement by Nisargadatta, whose name means "one who abides in the natural state," it was very liberating for me. It took a great weight off my mind. It was okay to still be human, even to experience occasional moments of fear.

Even great sages, established in truth for decades, are human, I realized. Their bodies fail them; they have their moments when the instrument, the body/mind, is not clear at all. They get indigestion; they may get irritated at times. They are not always so sweet and loving. They can be abrupt, aloof, or withdrawn. Their ordinary humanity gives us permission to be less than perfect ourselves, which takes a lot of pressure off us. Then we can relax more easily into the clarity and presence which is our true nature.

Jean spoke of these reactions from the past. He called them "residues," which is where I got the term. Liberation is seeing through the story called "me, myself, and I," so that you no longer derive your identity, or meaning, from your thinking processes or your personal history. Instead, it comes from *being* itself, from the fullness and vibrancy of the life force, the energy of creation felt right here, right now. You know yourself as consciousness, the changeless awareness in which the flux and flow of creation happens.

Once awakening happens, you are free. But elements of your personal history, those residues from the past, are still locked away in the musculature of your body. Any healer or body worker understands this phenomenon. It is similar to what the spiritual teacher, Eckhart Tolle, a master of the art of presence, refers to as the "pain body." These residues can get activated from time-to-time.

For instance, if you were impatient by nature before self-realization, there will still be residual tendencies toward impatience after you wake up, although much less often. Or if before awakening, you were afraid of confrontation, most of your fear will leave after you realize the truth of who you are. But should you then get into a confrontational situation, an echo from the past may be triggered. In other words, there may be a brief flaring up of fear.

The difference is, when you are awake, you notice it and it falls away. You don't buy into it any more. You don't give it energy and so it dissolves. Such upsets are like waves, momentary disturbances in the vast, clear ocean that is your natural consciousness, your natural state of being. Or, to use the lake analogy, the surface waters of your being may get upset when there is a strong wind, but deep down you remain still, clear, calm…

Pause right now and be present with whatever you are experiencing… Notice if you are feeling any tension or discomfort anywhere, whether mental, emotional, or physical… Accept it, let it be there… Notice the story you may be telling yourself… Then breathe, relax, and see

*the truth... The stories, thoughts, sensations,
and feelings are always changing, coming and
going...but "you," as the awareness witnessing
it all, are still* here... *You don't need, in this
moment, any story to define who you are...
You don't need any concept, image, or idea of
being "somebody"... You are aware of yourself
in reality right* now, *and that is enough... From
this place, everything happens...*

Beyond Duality

When I teach, I get variations of this question a lot: "I know awakening is often spoken of as nondual awareness, a freedom from the normal duality of everyday life. However, I don't understand how you can transcend duality. It seems to me that duality—night/day, good/bad, happy times/sad times—is reality. We live in a world of opposites, and you can't have the one without the other. You can't have the ups without the downs."

Obviously there is night and day, there is pleasure and pain, there is hot and cold, and there is wealth and poverty in the world, but even these distinctions are not clear-cut, not strictly black or white.

One person's pleasure is another person's pain, or at least discontent. Day gradually darkens into night, and in the morning, the dawning light heralds day-time once again. But in some parts of the world, in the polar regions, day lasts for twenty hours or more in the summer. Wealth and poverty are also a matter of perception. What we consider poverty here in the United States would be great wealth in some of the poorest Third World countries.

The main point of the question, above, is that we can't have the ups without the downs. That is true only when our happiness is based on events and circumstances outside ourselves. If you look to your partner for fulfillment, when your partner is happy and treating you well, you feel good. When your partner is unhappy and taking it out on you, treating you badly, you feel bad. You don't like the situation and it affects you adversely.

The same principle applies to everything else. When money is flowing in, it brings happiness. When more is going out than coming in, the result, in the words of Dickens' Mr. Micawber, is misery. Or maybe you are having deep, blissful experiences of meditation, which you label your "spiritual life," but your "material" life—your relationship, or your work—produces a lot of conflict and suffering.

So again, let me be very clear: If you are going to rely on external factors for your happiness and well-being, you will inevitably fluctuate between times of feeling good and times of feeling bad. You are caught in duality. You are a victim of duality. It can't be any other way.

Indeed, the more you depend on outer things for your happiness, the more likely you are to live with a chronic, underlying feeling of insecurity, never being quite sure when your good fortune may change or be taken away from you. This is the lot of most people, yet it needn't be this way.

When you live in the awareness, openness, and freedom of your true nature, your essential well-being no longer depends on outer events and circumstances, nor on what people think, say, or do. It comes from within. It shines through you as a direct expression of the beauty, fullness, and joy of *being* itself. Peace, in other words, is your true nature.

When awakening becomes real, you are always at peace within yourself, no matter what is happening outside. At the same time, you live in the world, in the dualistic reality. You are obviously going to make choices and act in such a way as to create the most optimal circumstances for your own survival, comfort, and well-being. The more smoothly your life works at a material, physical level, the freer you are to devote your energies to serving others and fulfilling your destiny.

You create positive karma. Karma is simply any action having reverberations, which results in a chain reaction. Positive karma is conscious action and generates feelings of love, compassion, and goodwill. Negative karma is caused by unconscious actions, and always results in suffering.

But again, the beauty of awakening, and why it is so important, is that your basic peace and well-being do not depend on whether outer conditions are favorable or not. It really does free you from being attached to, and thus at the effect of outer events, and the inevitable insecurity and suffering such attachment brings. It frees you from suffering because it frees you from the idea of being a "someone" who gets attached and who suffers.

I remember clearly the first taste of enlightenment, or awakening, I had. It was a truly life-changing event. Like all such awakenings, it came completely unbidden.

It happened a year after I graduated from Palmer College of Chiropractic, in Davenport, Iowa, and was living in Santa Rosa, in northern California. I had come to the United States to study chiropractic. I really wanted to be a writer, a novelist, but I liked the idea of helping people too, and thought chiropractic would be a good interim career. My plan after graduating was to return to New Zealand, establish a practice, write novels, and maybe get involved in politics, following in the footsteps of my paternal grandmother, who was the third woman elected to the Parliament in New Zealand.

During my last year at chiropractic school, I had a health crisis. I began getting tightness in my chest along with difficulty breathing. I was doing a series of breathing exercises, and had somehow gotten it into my head that if I didn't continue consciously controlling the flow of my breath, I would stop breathing altogether, and die.

This resulted in all kinds of anxious feelings. It got to the point where I was afraid to go to sleep at night. I'd sometimes make a feeble attempt at prayer, but I no longer really believed in God. I'd finally fall asleep from sheer exhaustion, and when I woke up the next morning, I'd give thanks for still being alive.

For me, it was a very unsettling time, a time of great personal distress. However, it takes this kind of suffering to cause us to look deeply within ourselves. I didn't realize it at the time, but my spiritual journey, my quest for inner freedom, had begun.

To deal with this situation, I started practicing yoga. When I went for my morning run, I stopped timing myself to see how fast I was going, and made a conscious effort to appreciate nature more, to actually stop and notice things, like the blue jay squawking in the apple tree, or the bees buzzing around the honeysuckle. I let go of trying to control my breath, and just started to trust more, to be more in the moment.

I took a course in Transcendental Meditation, and that made a big difference, stopping and sitting twenty minutes twice a day to just *be*. After a few months, the anxiety began to fade and I started to sleep well again.

As part of my quest for understanding I read the books of Herman Hesse, Alan Watts, and especially spiritual philosopher, J. Krishnamurti. As I dove into Krishnamurti's writings, I soon discarded whatever belief I still had in God altogether. Krishnamurti was, in many ways, the ultimate spiritual iconoclast. He said the prison of beliefs and concepts keeps us in bondage and causes all our suffering. Freedom, he said, lay in being free of the net of thoughts, of all concepts about God. Only then would we discover what was meant by the word "God."

It was a summer's morning when I had my taste of enlightenment. I woke up early and noticed a shaft of sunlight coming through a chink in the Venetian blinds. My gaze was transfixed by the dust motes dancing in the sunlight. Then I heard the soft, haunting call of a mourning dove, and suddenly everything in my mind fell away. Every thought, the residue of the night's dreams, it all just vanished and I lay there in the most extraordinary state of clarity, stillness, and oneness I had ever known. There wasn't even a sense of a "me" having the experience. There was just a feeling of timeless presence, and no tension or conflict whatsoever.

After a while, a thought entered my mind: "So, this is what Krishnamurti and all these other teachers are talking about. There is nothing to seek. It is all right here. Life is beautiful and perfect as it is."

As the day wore on, the amazing feeling of oneness faded and I gradually reverted to my normal, cerebral, somewhat uptight self. But something changed in me forever. It was as if a hole was punctured in my ego-bound consciousness. I tasted the Reality behind reality. At some level I realized I *was* that Reality. I glimpsed the divine perfection of creation, the beauty that is always here underneath the surface noise and conflict.

Now I knew what I was looking for. I wanted to live with that clarity, that sense of ease and oneness with life, all the time. I was totally committed and knew instinctively I was going to do whatever it took, to make whatever sacrifice was needed.

As a result of my inner commitment, I devoted the next eighteen years of my life to the pursuit of self-realization; to becoming fully established in the freedom I now knew was my true nature. Even as I outwardly lived a normal, worldly life, this became the central theme of my existence.

The Powerful Grip Of Personal Stories

Until we see them for what they are, the personal stories running us are many, and they are very deep-rooted. It takes time to ferret out our stories so we can see them for what they are: *just* stories, with corresponding emotional fallout in the body, but no substantial reality other than that.

There are stories of ambition and deprivation, need and want, desire and lust, greed and hunger, guilt and resentment, sadness and despair, hope and longing, friendship and betrayal, and so on.

These stories often have their origin in some form of personal trauma or abuse. It may be a psychological or emotional event which happened one or many times, or it may be a physical occurrence such as an illness, an accident, or some other calamity. Sometimes the psychological or emotional event also involves physical trauma.

Either way, we fabricate a story and a related "persona" (the personality we project) about what happened to us, and we gradually shut down. Over many years, the story and the persona become "us," become literally who we think we are. The intense feelings created by the story feel very real to us, and that just reinforces the importance of the story in our lives.

Let's take a closer look at some of the stories we tell ourselves, the stories keeping us separate from the flow of life, making us feel, to some degree, like victims of circumstance, or of life itself. Here they are, the bare-bones, stripped-down versions, without all the rationalization, justification, or personal narrative (which is just more "story") which usually accompanies them:

I'm not worthy, I feel guilty, I feel ashamed.
I am/was an abandoned, abused, wounded child.
Nobody would want to be with me.
Life is tough, unfair.
The only way you can get ahead is by ripping people off.
You can't trust anyone.
I don't manage money well.
I'd love to do such-and-such, but I won't because I'm not sure I would succeed.
He/she is my one chance for happiness.
I need/must have this or that (whatever the belief is) in order to be happy.
I'm too busy to take time for self-reflection/meditation.
I can't seem to get my mind to shut up.
I'm getting old. It sucks.
I really screwed up.
I'm confused/lonely/depressed/miserable.
I'm bored. I need something new and interesting to stimulate me.

The persona I spoke about above often becomes part of what psychologists call our "shadow self" because we have no conscious awareness of it. Only later, when we are triggered by something which reminds us of the original event, do we experience the drama associated with mental and emotional reactivity. We take offense, become angry, or feel any of the other sorts of human emotions: sadness, loneliness, depression, shame, guilt, and so on.

The shadow, in Jungian terminology, represents the unconscious aspects of your behavior, the things driving you of which you are not even aware. The shadow rears its head in what are sometimes referred to as "demons." Personal demons can manifest in many forms and guises, as I indicated above: fear, envy, jealousy, addictions, guilt, self-doubt, self-judgment, depression, despair, and phobias of various kinds.

The shadow is your disowned self. The more strongly you desire freedom, and the more closely you pay attention to your own thoughts, feelings, motives, and drives, the more you bring the shadow aspects into the light of awareness where you can see them. And it's in the seeing, the perceptual shift, that the healing happens.

You see it—your anger, for example—and you look for the story you are telling yourself, such as "How dare this person say—or do—this to me!" Then you breathe into the feeling. You stay very present, intensely alert. The stories, and the emotional reactions they trigger, are always changing, but you remember that *you* are the pure, changeless consciousness which is *looking* at the story. Remain in this place of awareness, and you'll find the images and feelings associated with anger dissolve, and a new energy of wholeness unfolds.

As another example of this perceptual shift, I remember many, many years ago a friend pointing out to me how judgmental I was about certain people. Perhaps it was because of the kind way in which she said it, but I had an epiphany: "My God, I *am* judgmental." Her observation literally stopped me in my tracks, and from that moment on, I became a lot less judgmental. In seeing the truth about myself, my judgmental tendencies toward others literally began to fall away.

Psychotherapy or some form of counseling or guidance is one way to get help in uncovering your shadow and coming to terms with the stories underlying your personal demons. Meditation, whether in the form of actual sitting, or just a very conscious, ongoing self-awareness, or self-inquiry, works well if you are highly motivated to find the truth within yourself. It requires a certain emotional maturity to do it on your own. You must have a passion for the truth, for freedom. You must be willing to confront your shadow, your demons, and find out just how real—or unreal—they are.

And, you must be patient, compassionate, and forgiving with yourself. Jean Klein always said the conditioning to be "somebody"—entrenched in your ego, with its obvious personal reactivity and its less obvious shadow self—is deep-rooted. Breaking free of the identification with the sense of "I," with the idea of a "me" living inside this body/mind, is the major hurdle to awakening.

We are convinced there is really "someone" in here, when in fact there is nobody. There is just consciousness, luminous, self-aware presence expressing through these body/minds and appearing as "us."

Awakening, or enlightenment, is a figure/ground shift, quite literally. You no longer take yourself to be an object, a "figure" amongst countless others. Instead, you now know yourself as the ground—as the ground of being, as consciousness. You know yourself as the ocean, manifesting as a wave, whereas before you just thought of yourself as one more wave, another separate human being, in the vast sea of consciousness. Once you really see that, you are free.

Occasionally I would meet people who were trying to free themselves from suffering through the direct, nondual approach, but who always seemed stuck in their heads. I felt they would have been better off spending a year or two working with a hands-on teacher who could actually reconnect them with their feelings and emotions. Sometimes catharsis, the actual expression of intense emotion, is necessary to get free of it.

Just before I met Jean Klein, I spent a year doing a series of intensive workshops with a transformational therapist named Stephano Sabetti. He was a master at working with emotional energy and at connecting people with their vulnerability. He got people to access their deeper, unexpressed emotions—their grief, anger, or fear—and invited them to release it, usually through catharsis or through acting it out in some way.

It was good work, what I call the "blood and guts" work of transformation. It made me much more emotionally available to hear Jean Klein's teachings on inner freedom. If you become a teacher or guide you can only take people as far as you have traveled yourself. If you have not dealt with your own anger, for example, you won't know how to be at ease with other people's anger when it comes up. You'll inadvertently draw angry students or clients to you and be at a loss as to how to work with them.

The main thing here is intention. If you have the clear intention to be open to whatever unresolved emotional energy still lives within you, then life will bring you what you need. That could be just the right guide or therapist; or maybe, because of what is happening in your relationships, you will experience it and release it on your own.

Just by inviting these inner demons to come up and encouraging them to show themselves, you initiate the process. The invitation, the welcoming, is the critical step in getting free of them. This is the ongoing daily meditation—this inner awareness of all that is taking place within you, of your own judgments, fears, unhappiness, resentments, your shadow side.

People who are still caught up in their story always have a shadow of some kind. Maybe it is the priest with his unresolved sexual longings for women or boys. Or maybe it is the woman who appears to be so kind and so well-mannered, yet turns vicious when she is crossed in any way. Maybe it is the husband who pretends to his spouse that everything is hunky-dory, yet whose dissatisfaction and resentment come out in passive aggressive behavior, in snide remarks and hurtful acts which only sabotage the relationship.

The way to be free of the shadow and its demons is to be very present. Begin to notice your behavior, your reactions, and the effect you have on people. It requires a commitment to self-honesty and to growth. You have to be willing to listen to the feedback your universe gives you, whether in the form of direct communication from others, or from the way people react to you. Looking at these deeper, darker aspects of ourselves is often not very pretty, but that's the gift of this work of welcoming. It is work which invites us to be easy on ourselves, to be forgiving. We cannot become free if we keep beating ourselves up.

It is the unconscious elements of your story, your beliefs and motivations, which control you. The more conscious you become of what lives inside you, the less power these forces have over you. Under the clear light of awareness directed within, guided by a loving and compassionate heart—and by a strong, warrior-like presence when needed—the shadow stuff is revealed. Because you are not giving it energy, it begins to fall away on its own. This is the transforming power of consciousness at work.

Residues of the shadow and those old demons may rear their head once in a while, but now you notice them, and you don't buy into them. You just don't go there anymore, because it doesn't serve you. Your awareness is right here, in the present.

Now, I am often asked about lessons, and why we have to keep learning the same old lesson. In every situation where there is suffering, there is a lesson to be learned. The work is to uncover the lesson and to find out what you are supposed to learn. Then, instead of being stuck in the same old story, the same old predicament, over and over again, you are able to profit from each lesson that comes along, and move on smoothly and easily to the next.

The quicker you let go of the attachment to your own story, and just listen and pay attention to what is so, the sooner you will be able to identify the lesson you are supposed to learn, and the closer you'll be to the freedom you seek. You'll then be more of a creative force in your life.

And if there isn't any story going on inside your head, but you are feeling emotionally contracted, or stuck, anyway, then you just do the practice. Let's do it right now…

Be present with the emotional contraction,
whatever it is… It is showing you where you

*are not yet free... (Maybe you aren't in touch
with the story behind it, but you can be sure
it is there, somewhere in your unconscious
mind)... Then breathe, relax, and notice how
the sensations of the contraction subtly shift and
change... But* you, *as the awareness watching
them, experiencing them, are always here...
So, remain as the clear, radiant, ever-present
awareness you are...*

At some level you will realize you are the clear, unchanging consciousness which looks at everything. You are the timeless awareness watching everything—your body, mind, and personality—come into being, including the ever-changing flow of your feelings and emotions.

Again, I want to emphasize there is *always* a story behind your suffering, though it may be unconscious. If you can find the story and see you are not the story, but rather what is *looking* at the story, then the shift can happen even quicker. After all, thought forms, which are ephemeral, dissolve virtually instantaneously when you, as the ultimate witness, just observe them. Contracted feelings and emotions, on the other hand, take longer to unwind.

Many people wonder about thoughts or stories which make them feel good, which don't cause emotional pain and suffering. For example, thinking about the new home you are going to move into, or the joy of graduating from college soon, or anticipating a new relationship, or something else great coming into your life. This is all pretty natural. These feel-good stories certainly do work to put a song in our hearts, and a smile on our face.

The thing is, to what extent are we identified with these stories? To what extent do we depend upon their outcome for our well-being? If the story becomes reality, then that is proof of the joy of anticipation. But sometimes anticipation is also expectation, and if our expectations are not met, we can be disappointed, sometimes bitterly so.

Remember, the essential message of this book is inner freedom. The freer you get inwardly, the less identified you are with any story, whether it's a suffering story or a feel-good story. Instead, you are more and more identified with *being* itself, with being here now. Feeling fully awake and alive in the present always feels very, very good. It feels the best. Moreover, the more you know you are *not* your story, the more fun it is to tell it. The freer you are of your story, the better story-teller you become.

In the mean-time, it is perfectly okay to indulge in a little feel-good story-telling, even a fantasy about something, now and then. This is a perfectly normal and human thing to do. Just don't mistake it for reality. To discover reality, be right here, right now, open to the fullness of this moment.

Compelling Religious Stories

The early stages of life are marked by the development of and identification with our ego, with our story, with the sense of "self." Most of us start out here. Ego development and the discovery of personal freedom, which includes boundaries and limits, is an important stage of learning in early life.

This stage is characterized by a dependence on—or a grasping at—beliefs. Our well-being is very much tied to what we think and believe. Our thoughts, our stories, define who and what we take ourselves to be. Religion and fundamentalist, black-or-white thinking in general, are a part of this developmental process.

In Zen, they say of this black-or-white stage, "Mountains are mountains, rivers are rivers."

Everything is just what it seems to be. The mountains are over there, and we are over here, just trying to make some logical sense of our existence. We are trying to find something to hold onto, some belief or concept or ideal—whether religious or otherwise—to give us a feeling of meaning, purpose, and security.

However, what drives us is precisely this need for meaning and security. Doubt, fear, and the quest for some kind of certainty are common themes in our lives. We realize we don't know who we are, or what is going to happen to us when we die. Or we find ourselves suffering in some way: an illness, financial misfortune, the loss of a job, the death of a loved one, or a betrayal of some kind, followed by broken trust and shattered confidence.

Our fear and suffering cause us to look for something to believe in, something we can cling to for our psychological, emotional, and spiritual well-being. We want to know the mountains and rivers are going to stay the same and will always be there. We want to know what is going to happen to us, both in the near future, and at the very end of our lives when we die.

This stage of the journey is very dualistic—"us" and "them," "me" and "it" (the thing we idolize or fear). It is very much a journey of faith as we hope or trust there is, indeed, some greater Power or benign energy—whether we call it God, spirit, Tao, or Buddha-nature—behind creation. So strong is this need that many of us develop a personal relationship with God, or whatever we call that power. We look to God—or our idea of God—whenever we are in need.

Some of us attribute the miracles in our lives to God's grace. Yet, we may wonder about disasters or times of extreme human suffering. What about when an airliner with 300 people aboard, crashes, killing everyone? Many of the dead probably had some form of "personal relationship" with God, How do we make sense of that? Can it be rationalized? Or do we accept it as a mystery? At this time in our journey through life, the last thing we want to be confronted with is that, in the end, we are just a random event in a cold and meaningless universe.

I grew up in New Zealand believing in God. When I was six years old, my mother taught me about God and Jesus. Although I was raised nominally as a Christian, I didn't particularly connect with the story of Jesus, but for me God became very real. There were times growing up when I would frequently stop and be still, look up at the sky, breathe into the beauty of the day, and definitely feel the presence of God, of a supreme and utterly benign power behind creation.

As I got older though, the whole idea of God became much less real for me. By the time I joined the army and arrived in Vietnam as a twenty-year old second lieutenant, serving with the Royal New Zealand Artillery, I was cocky enough to rarely think about God. But then I saw combat for the first time. Our unit came under attack from the Viet Cong. I found myself hugging the ground as bullets and rocket-propelled grenades flew overhead. Suddenly, fearing for my life, I was grateful to remember—and to call upon—the God I once knew so intimately.

Most people seek meaning in their lives, of course, and religion is there to provide it for them. The function of religion, at least in its outer, mass appeal aspect, is to address our existential fears and provide answers to these soul-searching questions of ours. Throughout history, man has created many religions, and they all have their own story, their own explanation of the nature of God, creation, and what happens to us when we die. Some religions even try to claim "God" as their own, as if theirs is the one true religion and all the others are false.

Religion still has a role to play, even in an awakened world, but religion in and of itself cannot give us the experience of authentic inner peace. After all, the main limitation of identifying with a particular religious story is that our inner well-being becomes very much dependent on what we think and believe.

We may adopt a particular set of beliefs, a neatly ordered worldview such as those offered by many religions, which are designed to give us the inner security we seek. But should someone (or something) challenge our beliefs or present a different or opposing perspective—and in a world as diverse as ours, this is always happening—it can throw us into confusion. It can, and inevitably does, throw us back into fear as the very belief system we have become dependent upon is now being called into question.

Beliefs, by their very nature, are divisive. They keep us in a state of resistance and fear. You can't cling to a belief *and* be in a state of "welcoming." Holding on to a set of beliefs is the exact opposite of the all-embracing openness represented by awakening. Not only do beliefs stir up conflict and doubt within us—"Which belief should I hold onto, which should I reject?"—they invariably create separation and rifts between one set of "believers" and another.

Most of the trouble in the world today is caused by the attachment to fundamentalist belief systems, whether religious, cultural, ethnic, or political. The more we see that all beliefs, including the most hallowed and emotionally charged ones, are just mental constructs—*assumptions* of truth, but not truth itself—the more we find ourselves wanting something deeper and more real than mere words and ideas.

The problem with religions is regardless of how long they have been around, how many adherents they have, or how noble or sacred their traditions, they are basically just stories about the origin, meaning, and purpose of life. And, as you are seeing, you are not your story, not any story.

Once you have seen through the illusion of the world inside your head you can no longer cling to any "story" about reality, including a religious story. Instead, you find yourself equally honoring the core of truth and goodness in all religions.

However, the path to freedom is not incompatible with attending church, or going to the mosque or temple. In fact, the freer you get of your own story and of attachment to ideas and images of "self," the more clearly you'll understand and relate to the heart of the great spiritual and religious teachings. You just won't get lost in all the dogma, rules, restrictions, and guilt-tripping.

Meister Eckhart, the fifteenth century German mystic, had clearly realized his true nature, but he continued to be a Christian preacher. The Dalai Lama is a contemporary example of an awakened human being who, because of destiny, finds himself speaking on behalf of Buddhism, Tibetan Buddhism in particular.

For a growing number of us throughout the world, however, the deeper our own inquiry into the true nature of God and creation, and the greater our own hunger for true inner peace and freedom, the less satisfied we are with attachment to any form of belief or story. We want the experience of freedom, of enlightenment, *now*.

For this to happen, we must be present in this moment now, see all our stories and beliefs for what they are—mere objects in consciousness—and realize what we *are* is the consciousness which sees…

> *Do it now… Be the consciousness you are… If it helps, step back with your awareness, out of any stories going on in your mind… Or, simply be present as the awake awareness you are… Then notice how you, as this aware being, are still here, shining through your eyes, feeling with your heart… Yet there is no need, in this moment, to define yourself by any story, whether religious, cultural, personal, or otherwise… There is no need to define yourself by any thought or concept… To realize this is to taste freedom, the freedom simply to be the beautiful, conscious person you are…*

The Consciousness Story

If there is a story that explains the true nature of reality, we could call it the consciousness story. This story is one of consciousness evolving *through* us, actually wanting to flower, to be born, through us. And the full flowering of consciousness happens when we realize that we are *That*; we are consciousness itself in human form. Then peace and wholeness become the reality within, and as more and more people awaken to the truth within, so peace and wholeness will eventually be the reality without.

Now, if you are able to put whatever beliefs and concepts you are still holding onto aside, and look at the way physical reality is put together, you will come to a remarkable discovery. You will come to the same insights arrived at by many leading-edge scientists in our own time.

This discovery is that reality is a unified field of energy and consciousness. It is not the universe of separate objects and things, of "us" in here, and the rest of the world out there, as Newton believed. It is a participatory universe, where every particle and every atom are interconnected. Physical reality is so interconnected that just by observing or looking into a system, you affect and change the system—and are, in turn, affected and changed by it.

This perspective brings an entirely new and astonishingly contemporary—and yet timeless—meaning to the Buddha's statements that, "Form is emptiness, and emptiness is form," and "All the ten thousand things are created by a single thought."

It allows us to hear Jesus' words, "I and the Father are One" in a new way, if you see "Father" as representing the consciousness we are. It makes it easier for us to understand Jesus when he said to his disciples (and I am paraphrasing his words here): "This applies to you, too. You are just as much a part of the Oneness as I am."

We are not separate from the rest of creation, but are one with it. Ramesh Balsekar, a contemporary Indian sage, reminds us that in Hindu mythology the universe was perceived thousands of years ago as a multi-dimensional net of jewels, each one a reflection of, and profoundly related to, the other. He quotes an ancient Chinese saying: "Pick a blade of grass and you shake the universe." And the fundamental quality connecting everything is consciousness itself.

Let me give you an example. Imagine you are sitting with a group of people by a lake. You come from different countries, different ethnicities, and you speak different languages. But the one thing you have in common is that you have all awakened to your true nature. Each of you knows yourself at the deepest level of your being.

So, it's a beautiful day, the sky is clear, and you are all sitting in total silence, in harmony with all existence. And what you become aware of is what you have always been aware of ever since first awakening to the truth within. You become aware there is only one consciousness present, expressing through each person—and all life—in unique and different ways.

Kunihiro Yamate, a contemporary Japanese social scientist and philosopher, says in *The Way of No Thinking*, a book describing his perspective on life:

"When we awaken to the fact that instead of being humans or earthlings we are universarians, we will have that indescribable realization that we are the thinker-uppers of the entire universe. The people we look at now are not others. They are mirror image reflections of our own self…

"Since we are mutually the whole universe, we can and should truly say: I am you, you are me. We have a holographic relationship. We are holographic beings and our dealings with each other are no longer individual-based. All us phenomena in the universe overlap. This is natural because we are all characters and props in a dream or play we are playing in our consciousness."

One thinks of the brilliant playwright, Shakespeare, in his own way a metaphysician, writing over four hundred years ago: "All the world's a stage, and all the men and women merely players."

What becomes clear with the universal or holographic view is we are scripting the whole thing. Nothing happens without our thinking or dreaming it into being. The personal proof of this is deep, dreamless sleep, where there is no awareness and no world. Yet when you start dreaming, the dream world is very much there because you are aware of it. Then, when you wake up, the "real" world is here, because you are aware of *that*.

The more deeply you grasp this perspective, the more it transforms your understanding of who you are, what God is, how you have come to be here, and what happens to "you" when your body dies.

As you open to these deeper levels of reality, it dawns on you that consciousness itself—pure, radiant awareness—*is* your true and abiding nature. And if consciousness is your true nature, if consciousness is the primary force behind creation, then consciousness—the clear, undifferentiated consciousness expressing not just through the human brain/mind, but through all of creation—must be God.

In other words, the universe is God. God is the whole thing. God is consciousness itself and "you," as this body/mind/self, are an individualized, unique expression of the one divine consciousness.

Understanding this, not just at an intellectual level but with the whole of your being, so there is no longer any feeling of being separate from the flow of consciousness and creation, is the essence of what it means to be awake or free.

In this freedom, you use the power of stories and of thoughts *consciously*, because you know how powerful the mind is. You use thoughts intentionally to create the reality which best supports you and the people you love—and best supports the environment.

With this freedom you experience a natural sense of oneness and unity, and this gives rise to a heightened sensitivity and compassion toward all of life. Above all, you experience a deep inner peace and silence.

This is the secret realized by all who venture beyond their identification with the "I" thought. They discover the vast realm of *being* lying beyond the mind, and yet which is the source of the whole of creation, which includes the mind and the "I" thought.

Releasing Stories Around Fear

One of the traditional definitions of awakening, or enlightenment, is it is a state of fearlessness.

The journey of awakening is above all a process of

uncovering and facing your different fears. As you see with more and more clarity that they are not real, they begin to fall away. Then you are naturally more loving and more connected to consciousness, God, spirit, or whatever you choose to call the mysterious Power behind creation.

Together, the teaching and the practice equip you to face and move through your fears, eventually leaving them all behind you. Instead of shrinking from fear and turning it into some kind of monster, you meet it head on, like a warrior, and discover its real face. There's an old Irish saying: "If you run away from a ghost, it will chase you and haunt you for the rest of your life. But if you stop and turn and face it, it will disappear, because ghosts aren't real."

On the path of awakening, you are learning to face not just fear, but every moment, in this alert and relaxed way. Years ago on my own journey, whenever I had a breakthrough, I found myself coming to the same realization every time. It involved letting go of some aspect of my past, my story—some pattern in my thinking or behavior which no longer worked for me.

Suddenly, I'd feel more relaxed, more *here*. I would say to myself: "Wow, my spiritual journey is all about getting here. It's about being more present."

You can probably relate to what I am saying. As you grow up and get caught up in your personal story, the account you inwardly write of your life, of your history of failures and successes, doubts and fears, hopes and dreams, you tend to start dwelling in this internal reality. You are not alone. We all do this until we learn differently. Yet it is the very attachment to this inner world of concepts, beliefs, memories, and images that keeps us from being present.

The deeper your awakening, the freer you get of psychological and emotional fear. You no longer worry about what *might* happen to you. You know now that you, as consciousness, will always be okay.

But even with awakening, biological fear, the fear of actual physical harm, still arises when danger threatens. It is a necessary survival mechanism. If someone moves as if to strike you, you are going to flinch or jump back. If you take up sky-diving, even if your realization is deep and mature, chances are your stomach will feel nervous and queasy as you are about to step out of the airplane at ten thousand feet.

But even survival fear loses its edge as you awaken to the consciousness you are and connect with the astonishing creative energy which is always here, underneath the surface drama of life.

The more conscious and free you become, the more you find even in the face of danger, hardship, or loss, you remain clear-headed and supremely aware as you deal with the situation at hand. When you stop resisting and fighting it, life has its own surprising way of coming into balance and harmony. This is how miracles occur. It all happens not in some promised future or some imagined after-life, but right now, in this present moment.

Rather than obsessing over what it takes to become enlightened, why you still suffer, or why you are not yet free, let go of the attachment to all your ideas and stories about enlightenment and suffering, and just focus on being fully aware, conscious, and present *now*. Then the experience of freedom will become more and more frequent, and the times of conflict and suffering will be fewer and briefer.

Eventually, as your internal gaze penetrates more deeply through the illusion of the world between your ears, the world you have for so long been referring to as "me, myself, and my story," all fear of life and death will leave you. Then the liberation you have been seeking will be yours.

The Practice Of Looking For The Story

Sit in meditation for a few minutes and observe your body, your breathing, sensations, thoughts, and feelings within the awareness you are... Now recall the most recent incident when you were shaken or rattled, when your buttons were

72

pushed, when you found yourself stewing over something or suffering in some way.

Then simply be present with the memory. You can even welcome it, and affirm to yourself: "Ah, this is showing me where I am not yet free."

Now look for the story you told yourself immediately prior to the upset. Something happened, or someone said or did something, or you thought about something, and it triggered a reaction in you. It violated some deep-rooted belief or idea—your "story"—about the way things should be or ought to be. The consequence was upset and suffering.

Then, from this more relaxed, meditative place, see how it was simply the story that caused the emotional reaction in you. Maybe the story arose from some rejection or hurt which happened to you far back in your past. You made up a story about it, and it's been running you ever since. This process may bring up other stories, other emotions, fears, and insecurities. Be present with them, too...

Notice how the story, thought, or belief you tell yourself shifts and changes, and the feelings and sensations you experience also shift and change. Then see the truth... You, as the awareness or witness watching it all, are always here. You don't change. Only the contents of your mind, and the feelings in your body, change...

If the situation triggering the upset is liable to happen again, you can visualize it in your mind. Imagine the worst-case scenario. See it happening.

Then say to yourself: "What if this were to happen to me again? How would I respond to it if I were already free?" Then gently come back to being the clear, vibrant awareness you are.

This is an especially powerful way to work through your fear of death. What if you were about to die? What else can you do but be supremely present, to face it with open eyes, so to speak? This is how a true warrior faces his or her last living moment—without any story—and you are learning to do the same.

You are developing the presence that will allow you to face all your fears and see their fundamental unreality. Your fears are just stories and pictures inside your head, with corresponding reactive feelings in your body. Who and what you really are is far, far bigger than anything you are experiencing.

As you illuminate these stories, beliefs, and images with the power of presence, with the clear light of your consciousness, they will dissolve. The contracted feelings will expand, and you will open up to the boundless clarity and freedom of your true nature.

Chapter Three

Step 3—See The Truth

The heart of the teaching is seeing you are not your story. Rather, you are what is *looking* at the story—clear, vibrant, present-time consciousness. To make this real, you must practice being very present, very vigilant as you go through your day.

Eventually, you will come to realize you are the ultimate witness of everything you observe. You are the awareness, or consciousness, which notices your body, mind, personality, *and* the stories you tell yourself.

Such vigilance has vast rewards. When you truly see you are not your story, not *any* story, a shift will happen. You will find that stories lose their power over you and emotional upset and conflict dissolve, thereby freeing up your energy. You feel more centered and grounded in your true being, in pure consciousness itself. You literally see everything with new eyes. You can deal with what's before you with clarity and strength.

Now, a question I am sometimes asked is this: "I see the power of the shift you are talking about, yet I feel reluctant to let go of the religious story I grew up with. I guess I have lingering fears from my Catholic (or Protestant, or Jewish, etc.) upbringing. I am afraid of God's judgment, and of falling short of pleasing Him."

Our inner, spiritual journey only truly begins when we start the process of questioning the personal, cultural, and religious stories we have become so identified with, including our concepts around God, and our fear of judgment.

The journey is a process of letting go of attachment to our inner conceptual reality as we seek, through silence and stillness, to find something beyond words and ideas, beyond our concepts and beliefs around "God." It can be an unsettling time in our lives, because we are calling into question everything we've held most dear. Everything upon which we have built our personal sense of identity begins to come undone.

With deep self-examination, doubt and skepticism enter the picture, and we are no longer sure what to believe. We are no longer sure of who or what we are. In Zen they say of this questioning phase: "Suddenly mountains are no longer mountains, rivers are no longer rivers."

This stage of our spiritual unfolding is a time of learning to be comfortable with *not* knowing, the necessary precursor to the attainment of true knowledge, or insight. This phase can involve a lot of "dark night of the soul" experiences. These occur when all our inner fears, demons, and doubts build in intensity, and we feel as if there is absolutely nowhere to turn, least of all to a "God" in whom we have lost faith. Yet it is a perfect opportunity to develop our skill in the practice, in our ability to stay present and open to all of existence, in the face of self-doubt and uncertainty.

Here, our religious yearnings deepen and flower into true spirituality. Spirituality is religion made personal and experiential. Religion emphasizes beliefs, codes, doctrines, and the need for intermediaries—the priest, the pastor, the rabbi, the mullah—between us and the divine. Spirituality is characterized by letting go of beliefs and concepts, and opening to a more direct *experience* of the unity and joy which religion talks about.

This, of course, is after we have confronted, through the power of our own presence and unwavering awareness, whatever demons or dark nights may be assailing us. It requires us to be vulnerable, open to whatever is arising. At some point, most of us have to walk through our own personal fire, sometimes even a raging inferno of emotion, fear, or self-doubt, before we come to stillness and peace. It is perhaps no wonder someone once said: "Religion is for people afraid of going to hell; spirituality is for people who have already been there!"

If the religious stage of the journey is based on "believing" (or trying to believe) in some version of truth, or in whatever story about God and creation most appeals to us, this phase is where we start to actually know the truth for ourselves. Letting go of what we "think" we know, our awareness expands, and we begin to really *know*—to sense, in a deep and discernable way—the immensity and timelessness of the consciousness which is our true nature.

In moments of stillness we can feel this consciousness as an actual energy, a flow, a powerful sense of mystery and presence. And this is where we find our faith: in the palpable nature of existence, rather than in stories, beliefs, and ideologies.

When you find yourself being caught up in your head, in some story you are telling yourself, this is your signal to take a deep, slow breath, relax, and *be* present. Do the practice. Become very aware of what you sense and feel within and around you. Welcome, allow, whatever is arising in your experience. This is what it means to be a conscious human being.

Remind yourself of this often: you are *not* your story about who you are or what is happening. You are the ever-present consciousness, the timeless awareness witnessing, experiencing, and participating in the unfolding of creation.

The more you look within, the more you literally dive into the well of your own being—and it is here, in the depths of your own heart and soul, where you discover the true source of well-being. The deeper you go into the present moment, the more likely you are to touch the bliss all spiritually awake people have discovered, regardless of religion, tradition, or lineage…

Do it now. Pause and be present for a few
moments… Notice any thoughts or stories going

*on in your mind, and affirm: "I am not my
story..." Then breathe, relax, and be present...
Drop into the now... Then, from this place of
clarity visualize, internally, the vastness which
is your true nature... The vastness manifesting,
when you are one with it, as bliss in every cell of
your being... Breathe into this bliss... Relax into
it... Then open your eyes, and be fully present,
here, now...*

Bliss arises with knowing, through direct experience, that you really are a manifestation of the one divine energy or consciousness. You are a part of the loving force which births, nourishes, sustains, and guides the universe. This power is the source of all creation. When you know yourself as this power, the names we have traditionally given it don't really matter. As the *Tao Te Ching* says: "The Tao which can be named is not the Tao. If names be needed, wonder names it."

You may not be deeply established in this knowing yet. Maybe you often lose the sense of connectedness and of unity. Maybe you still feel somewhat separate from the underlying flow of life. Maybe you hold to the idea of the witness, of being the dispassionate observer of the arising thoughts, feelings, and emotions, and this produces a certain dryness within you. This is inevitable.

Attaching to any concept or story, especially if it goes on for many years, always results in squeezing out the juice or extinguishing the passion from the moment-by-moment experience. Or maybe you go back and forth between peaceful, blissful meditative states and personal conflict, self-doubt, and resistance to what is.

Now for many, many people, just to touch the divine in this way is enough, and they go no further. They find a home in their chosen religion or practice. They live in relative peace and harmony.

But for those seekers who hunger for full realization—as

I did, and as you, reading this, probably do as well—relative peace and harmony is not enough. We want nothing less than for consciousness to awaken fully within us. By the time we get deeply into our inner journey, the barrier separating us from the realization of our true nature—our attachment to our story, to our beliefs, judgments, assumptions, prejudices, expectations, and desires—is becoming thinner and more transparent.

What takes us into the final phase of the journey is what fueled the hunger driving us to embark upon this questioning and seeking: the longing for true freedom.

Desire

Many people assume that awakening is synonymous with freedom from desire, but it is actually not being *attached* to desire. People who are awake are still living, breathing, feeling human beings. They still have desires and preferences, but the difference is that they are not attached to them. Consequently, they don't suffer. They don't experience disappointment, frustration, or anger when the desire is not fulfilled—or, if they do, it is only momentary, and they come back to their normal way of being, flowing with what *is*, very quickly.

Thomas Merton, the 20th Century Trappist monk who was also keenly interested in Eastern wisdom, said: "The only desire not a sin is the desire for God."

Knowing that God is synonymous with awakening, or true inner freedom, you must want it more than you want anything else. That's the deal. You must want it more than you want money, power, fame, sex, relationships, or any of the seemingly infinite number of things human beings seek in order to find security, happiness, and fulfillment in their lives.

To desire these other things is not "wrong" in any moral sense, but it is a "sin" as Merton points out. The original Greek meaning of sin is "to miss the mark." A sin, then, is any action or behavior taking us away from the only place where authentic, lasting peace and happiness can be found: within the depths of our very own being, within our God-nature.

This is precisely why awakening continues to elude most people. They have been seduced by the media, movies, television, and popular magazines into thinking happiness lies "out there" somewhere. We are programmed to believe happiness lies in having more money, a bigger house, a more expensive car, a whiter smile, a thinner body, a prettier girlfriend, a more successful boyfriend, and so on.

There is nothing wrong with having any of these things in and of themselves. It's the *attachment* to them which creates all the suffering. If you make these things the sole focus of your life, you'll never find the deep happiness and freedom of your inner nature.

In this regard, Nisargadatta Maharaj said: "Enlightenment may seem arduous, but it is easy if you are earnest, and quite impossible if you are not. Everything yields to earnestness."

Intention, which is earnestness with a focus, is fundamental to attaining anything worthwhile in life. Look at people who are successful in the world in every other sense, whether it's in politics, business, sports, entertainment, or just making money for its own sake. Such people are strongly motivated by their desires and have very clear goals. They pursue their goals with their whole heart and mind. They want to achieve their objectives more than they want anything else, and they are willing to make whatever sacrifice is necessary.

Awakening or enlightenment is no different. You must want it with your whole heart and mind. Yet there's a paradox here, too, because you must let go of the wanting at the same time. If you become too obsessed with getting enlightened, in the sense that you are always thinking about it, it gets in the way of your ordinary, daily life. You develop an unrealistic view of what enlightenment is. You develop a story about it. You can get so caught up in the pursuit of whatever you imagine enlightenment to be, you end up not dealing with such real-world issues as working, paying the rent, taking care of business. You end up not being present.

How to balance the deep desire with letting go? I like the

mountain climbing analogy I read about in Robert Pirsig's *Zen And The Art Of Motorcycle Maintenance*, in which he describes how a Zen master climbs a mountain. The master is determined to reach the summit, which, in our case, is a metaphor for awakening. He then lets go of the goal, puts it in the back of his mind, and focuses on enjoying the journey.

So it is with you. You remember that awakening is your ultimate goal, but that the ongoing work is to be truly aware and present each and every moment of the day. When you start getting caught up in your story, in your beliefs, concepts, justifications, excuses, judgments, and rationalizations, notice it. Notice it, then breathe and come back to the present, to the awareness of your true nature.

Come back to the awareness of yourself as the consciousness which gives birth to the entire universe, expressing through this body, mind, and heart called "you." Come back to enjoying the journey.

Letting Go Of The Story

Awakening is the result of releasing one's story, of releasing all beliefs, concepts, and images of "self" and opening up to the beauty and power of the present moment. It is letting go of the attachment to the *forms* of consciousness—thoughts, emotions, experiences—and finding your identity in the formless ground of being itself.

This releasing happens naturally when you see that the story—this internal drama you have been so identified with all these years—is not even real. Then you are awakened into the timeless present.

In a workshop once, a woman said to me: "How can you say my story is not real? As a child, I was physically and emotionally abused by my stepfather, and my mother did nothing to stop it. Even now, at the age of forty, I still have strong memories of those years. Sometimes I have nightmares about them."

I responded that the experience of being abused as a child, in her case, was undoubtedly real when it happened, and repeated abuse over many years certainly reinforces a "story" of anxiety, victimhood, and suffering.

As long as you keep telling yourself the story—for example, "My horrible childhood scarred me for life"—then it will continue to generate feelings of pain and numbness, of grief and fear. You will indeed feel scarred to some degree, and this emotional scarring may affect your ability to function as a mature, responsible adult.

When people do have this kind of heavy emotional wounding from the past, it does seem very much as if the person "is" their story. Such people often need some intensive, long-term psychotherapy in order to begin to heal their past and free themselves from it. But no matter how psychologically or emotionally wounded you were back then, it was in the past, and this is now. There is no person abusing you now. If there is, the wise thing would be to remove yourself immediately from that person's company.

If you want to be free of suffering, then you must begin to look within. You must see it as the identification with your story—the attachment to your memories from the past—which keeps retriggering pain and hurt in the present.

In other words, you believe the past matters, so you get lost in the forms of the past. But the memories, stories, and beliefs you hold onto, no matter how true you might insist they are ("I had a rotten childhood," "I'm not worthy," "My mind, with its haunting memories, won't shut up") only serve to prevent new creative and healing possibilities from revealing themselves to you.

The more you learn to be present, expand your awareness, and see the entire inner drama for what it is—a self-generated "story," a mish-mash of thoughts, beliefs, and perceptions which cannot actually be found anywhere, other than in your mind—the more it all drops away. Without the psychological and emotional holding your body relaxes, your mind clears, and you start to awaken to the experience of your true nature as openness, spaciousness, and freedom.

However, even though freedom is realizing you are not your story, you still have a story. We all have a story. We all have many stories. One of the delights of being human is this ability we have to share our stories. We have stories of our history and culture; stories of the things we have built, dreamed, or imagined; stories of our successes, failures, mistakes, and lessons; and stories of our loves, losses, joys, sorrows, and despair.

The beauty of awakening is that as you release attachment to and identification with the stories you have used to describe who you are, you are then able to live with them and talk about them without personally suffering over them. This makes them a lot more fun and enjoyable—and, yes, sometimes poignant and sad. At the same time, because you are no longer caught up in all the drama around them, you are able to learn whatever lessons you need to learn much more effectively and speedily.

The quicker you let go of the attachment to your own story, and just listen and pay attention to what *is*, the clearer you will get about any lesson you are supposed to learn, and the closer you'll be to the freedom you seek. Then you can begin to write a new story for your life, except now you will be doing it consciously, without the personal identification or attachment.

Drop All Philosophies

Until you actually awaken to deeper levels of freedom, it's inevitable that you will try to hold onto a story—some thought, belief, concept, or philosophy—which gives you the flavor and feeling of the freedom you seek. This is okay up to a point, but eventually it will become clear to you that even the words and philosophies, no matter how accurate or succinct they may be, have to be released.

One of the last public talks I attended with Jean Klein was in a church hall in Sausalito, California. There were fifty or sixty people in the room, waiting patiently for Jean to come in and take his seat at the front. When he arrived, he had to be helped to his chair. He seemed very old, thin, and frail, yet his gracious European bearing was still very much in evidence, and he was dressed as elegantly as ever.

He sat down with some difficulty and smiled at us. A beautiful, clear light emanated from his eyes. We sat in silence for a while, and then he began to speak. He talked of the need to see through the "person" so we could come to our real presence, our true being. There were some questions, and subsequent dialogue. About half-way through the evening, a serious-looking young woman in a business suit raised her hand. When Jean acknowledged her, she stood up. She looked like a banker, or a stockbroker.

"Dr. Klein, may I ask, what is your philosophy of life?"

There was a long silence. Then Jean beamed one of those disarming smiles of his. "Madame, I have no philosophy... That is why I am a happy man."

Laughter rippled throughout the room. The young woman smiled rather self-consciously, and then sat down.

For months after the exchange, I found myself thinking about Jean's words. It was so simple. Forget the philosophies, the stories, the beliefs, the theories and just abide in the openness and freedom of our true nature. Then we really will be happy. We'll live out of wholeness, with wisdom and compassion, and we'll do what needs to be done—without fuss, without bother.

But if we hold onto a philosophy, a belief system, or an agenda of any kind, we create a barrier to the unfolding of something deeper, something more authentic, fresh, and alive. When our beliefs reinforce the idea of being a separate "self," a lonely wave on the ocean of life, it is that separation that breeds feelings of isolation, insecurity, and fear.

But when we let go of all philosophies, all stories, and just *be*, happiness is ours...

See if you can touch that place right now... Be present with whatever you are experiencing... Notice any thoughts or stories passing through your mind, and any sensations of feelings in

your body, and see them for what they are...
Just passing phenomena, coming and going...
Now visualize yourself as empty space on the
inside of your body, an emptiness which is at the
same time infinitely full... Notice how "you,"
as the one who is aware of all this, are still
very much here... In this moment, you need no
story or philosophy to define you... Then open
your eyes and just be present as the beautiful,
conscious person you are...

Lose Your Head

One morning, a year or two before I finally awakened to the freedom that is our true nature, I was meditating on the deck outside the small country cottage where I used to live. My mind was a little bit noisy, my thinking cloudy. I wasn't feeling totally aligned in body, mind, and spirit. There was a certain ease missing. As I sat on my meditation cushion and looked eastward, over the richly verdant hills and valleys to the mountains beyond, the words came to me:

Supremely present, mind still,
I breathe in the beauty of this moment.

This *mantra* worked for me many times over the years. For me it always held a special power, a reminder to be present. Anyway, I became very still, very alert, with all my senses engaged. Then suddenly my head pierced through the scattered gray clouds of thought still in my mind, and my awareness became like the morning sky itself—vast, pristine, and empty. Everything was stunningly, vibrantly clear.

I say it was as if my head pierced through the clouds, but when I noticed my body, it was as if I didn't have a head. Above my shoulders there was only awareness, openness, a boundless clarity and radiance... And it was streaming with the world around me... The sky itself, the trees and the valley nearby, the mountains in the distance, the occasional crow flying by, a turkey vulture circling lazily overhead, all became one.

It was the strangest experience, and wholly illuminating. It was the first time I saw that everything between my ears was unreal. The stories aren't real. Thought is unreal. The pictures and images passing through the mind are unreal. They are just phantoms, ephemeral flashes, momentary appearances which may have a symbolic or creative value, but have no separate reality in and of themselves.

As I sat there, breathing into the extraordinary feeling and freedom of being "headless," I remembered a book I'd read many years before, by the English mystic Douglas Harding. It was called *On Having No Head*. In it he describes an experience similar to mine which resulted in him realizing his true nature.

One day he was hiking in the Himalayas and everything in his mind suddenly stopped. He looked down at his legs, passed his gaze upwards to his shirt-front, and found a hole where his head was supposed to be. But the hole wasn't just empty: it was filled with the vastness of the Himalayan panorama all around him. In his words, "I had lost a head and gained a world."

Throughout the day, periodically contemplate the notion that the world you've created between your ears is unreal— including your sense of "self," of being a "somebody" with a personal history. This practice alone will bring you, sooner or later, to the headless state. In seeing that thought has no substantial reality, your head will start to clear.

Instead of having this solid, round, bowling ball-like "thing" which worries, frets, and obsesses sitting on your shoulders, you'll start to experience a lightness, a spaciousness, a wonderful sense of emptiness and freedom where your head used to be.

The experience of headlessness brings you into your body, into your heart. It dissolves the illusion of fear and opens the door to love. As you begin to live more fully in your body, in your natural state of awareness, sensation, and feeling, you won't need a conceptual identity. You won't need to cling to stories and beliefs, to a "self" image of any kind.

You'll use thinking as the creative instrument it is, but you won't be controlled by it.

You'll awaken to who and what you really are. The current of energy or spirit behind all creation will become a tangible presence for you. This will be all the proof you need of your own existence.

This ability to actually feel the beauty and power of the energy you are made of will be all the evidence you need of your life being inherently meaningful and worthwhile.

Loneliness And The Void

A forty year old man once shared with me: "I am going through a very difficult time. Whenever I sit to meditate I get to a point where I start to feel a sense of peace, of well-being. And then, from somewhere deep inside me, a thought or image floats up having to do with my family, my friends, or my work, and it produces a feeling of anxiety.

"It makes me feel as if I am on the wrong path, and instead of bringing me more into life, meditation is somehow cutting me off from it. I find myself suddenly feeling very alone in the universe—achingly alone. It feels like this terrible void, and panic sets in. I have to immediately think about something positive, or stop meditating altogether. What should I do about this?"

Many, many years ago I went through something very similar. Like this man, I would sit and meditate, get to a certain depth of relaxation, and then an awful sense of emptiness, of the void, would loom. In my case, this went on for well over a year. It got to where I was almost afraid to sit and meditate any more.

Then, in 1982, I attended a retreat led by Richard Moss in southern California's high Mojave Desert. Richard was a former medical doctor who became a transformational teacher. His work had a major impact on me at the time. He taught me to get out of my head, out of the realm of thought, and awaken to energy, sensation, feeling, to the nonverbal elements of experience.

As the retreat began, I made a pact with myself: for the next ten days I wouldn't try to intellectually understand the experiences I went through. I'd been experimenting with a new kind of awareness in my life and discovered how powerful it was just to be in the *experience* of whatever was happening, without the interference of the conceptual, analytical, story-making mind.

It turned out to be an extraordinary ten days, with many peak experiences, insights, breakthroughs, emotional highs, and a few lows. Then, on the last evening, about an hour before we were to attend our final dinner, I decided to meditate for a bit. I bundled up, for the night was cold, went out into the darkness, and sat on the porch of my cabin. It was utterly quiet and still. Above me, the night sky was black and immense, carpeted with the brilliant light of myriad stars. In the valley stretching out before me were a few scattered lights from the ranches in the area. Beyond the valley were the rugged mountains, darkly silhouetted against the night sky.

As I sat I began to get very still. At first there was peace, a gentle letting go of the tension I'd been carrying in my body from a long hike I'd taken that afternoon. But as I became more still, "it" began to happen again: the haunting emptiness and loneliness plaguing my meditations started to descend like a dark cloud. I found myself thinking of my parents who lived far, far away, in New Zealand, and of a brother who lived in Australia. I wondered whether I would ever see them again. Being in the desert, in the dark, barren emptiness, just magnified what I was feeling.

Suddenly, I'd had enough. I didn't want to meditate any more. I didn't want to be a solitary seeker of truth. I didn't want to be enlightened. It was too lonely. It brought up too much fear, the fear of the unknown. I told myself I would think about something else, something normal. I'd had enough of cutting myself off from life in this way.

But something within told me not to run off into my

mind, just to stay with the emptiness, to be very present with it. I remembered some words Richard quoted from the Bible: "Exalt the valleys." The message was to embrace whatever was happening.

Several years later I heard Jean Klein say the same thing, but in different words: "Welcome your experience." The idea was not to run from whatever was happening, but to face it. To be supremely present with it, and not get lost in any story—not get into your head—about it.

In facing it and trusting it, the feeling or sensation undergoes a transformation and becomes something else. This is the way to freedom. In my case, I realized it was fear I was running from, especially the fear of not-being, the fear of "Who am I without my story?"

So, it was an innate trust, something deeper within me, which now whispered, "It's all right, Jim, this emptiness is showing you where you're not yet free. Let it be your friend. Don't reject it. You've been running from it for a long time. Why don't you just be with it?"

So I breathed slowly and deeply into every part of my body. Then I looked up at the cold night sky again, the brilliant stars. They seemed to take on a friendly twinkle. When I turned my attention within again, I found the emptiness was still there, but somehow it didn't feel quite so empty. The edge had been taken off. It didn't make me anxious as it did before.

After a while I got up and went down to join the others for dinner. It was a happy evening, a celebration of all we'd been through together, and there was much joy and laughter. During the evening I occasionally checked inside to see what I was feeling. The emptiness was hardly there. It was more like a vaguely felt memory.

After that desert retreat, the emptiness never came back again, at least not with any force behind it, and I was able to go to new depths in my meditations. When it did surface, I'd just face it, accept it, and breathe into it. It would always diminish and eventually dissipate. You'll find the same freedom too, if you learn to exalt the valleys and to welcome even the so-called negative experiences. Don't run from fear and it will become your friend.

No matter what you are experiencing, no matter what the sensation, feeling, or emotion, be very present with it. Treat it as a residue of the past. There is nothing to get upset about, so breathe into it and let your awareness expand. Don't get into your head, into some story about what is happening. If it helps, tell yourself: "Ah, I welcome this feeling. It is showing me where I am not yet free." Or you can just say, "This too shall pass," as it will. Then open yourself to it.

Open yourself not just to the residue of anxiety or fear, but to all you are aware of in this moment. Breathe deeply and be very present. Remember what you are here for: to awaken, to be free.

Do this, and the energy will shift. It will come into harmony. Then you will know the peace of your true nature. You will have a direct experience of it, and it won't depend on anything, not on any story, belief, condition, or circumstance.

"How Do I Hold Onto This?"

One of the most common questions I am asked by people who have tasted their true, timeless nature is: "How do I hold onto this peace, harmony, or bliss I am feeling?" Of course the answer is you can't hold onto it, because it is what you fundamentally *are*.

It is only when "you," as pure awareness or consciousness, see through the illusion of the ego, the little, mind-made "me" who wants to try and maintain the peaceful or blissful state, that you relax into the ease and spaciousness of your natural state of being.

Earlier, I spoke of Suzuki-Roshi, and how he said it was important to have a beginner's mind. Beginner's mind is not something you acquire. It is your natural state of being. To return to it, let go of all the knowledge and all the stories you have accumulated, even if only for a minute or two, and just be very present in this moment. Be aware of yourself *as* the awareness, the consciousness behind everything. Do this and you are in beginner's mind. Then there will be no question about holding onto anything. You will simply be in the flow, at peace, one with life.

Let me tell you another Zen story which speaks exquisitely about this practice of beginner's mind. Two monks were strolling down a path toward a river. The older one was an enlightened master. The other monk was much younger, but still a sincere seeker. As they drew near the water, they came across a young woman who, by her manner, was evidently distressed.

"I must get over the river without getting my kimono wet, but the recent rains have made it too deep for me to cross," the woman said. She looked at the two monks. "I have to visit the parents of my fiancé. Will you please carry me? I would be most grateful."

"By all means," said the master, beckoning the younger man to help with lifting her. The young monk hesitated, frowning, but then held out his hands. Together, they made a seat out of their four clasped hands, and carried the young woman safely across.

"Thank you," she said, as she stepped onto the dry ground, gave a gracious bow, and went on her way.

The two monks walked off. After they walked a few miles the younger man, who had been internally stewing since the moment they stopped to help the woman, turned to the older monk.

"I don't understand it, Master," he said. "According to the rules of our monastery, we are not supposed to even talk to young unmarried women, let alone touch them."

"Ah," said the master, turning to the younger man, "You're still carrying her… I put her down by the river."

This has always been one of my favorite Zen teachings. Zen is a philosophy or spiritual path with its own set of traditions, rules and regulations. Yet Zen masters throughout history have been notorious for breaking them. They understand rules are meant to serve as guidelines only. In this story, the master was being guided by his heart, not his head. The young woman needing help took precedence over the rules about touching unmarried women. So, for him, there was no hesitation in providing assistance.

The attachment to wanting something to believe in, some principle, rule, or understanding to hold onto in order to feel a sense of security is always strong at the beginning of the spiritual journey. However, such attachment invariably gets in the way of our responding intelligently, creatively, and lovingly to the very real needs of the present moment. Opening up to a deeper level of freedom and happiness in the present begins with the deliberate releasing of whatever you are holding onto from the past.

As you learn to put your baggage down, to empty your mind in this way, a tremendous gathering of energy happens, because it is no longer being fragmented or dissipated by thought. You find yourself being very aware in the present.

In this state of awareness and openness, thinking is liberated from all the psychological and emotional overlays, and is available as a powerful creative tool—a tool for wise and compassionate action.

Let Go Of Your Attachment To Bliss

Like the question about holding onto the awakened state, I hear variations of this quite often: "When I started my own spiritual journey many years ago, I was moved by a burning desire not just for my own freedom, but I really wanted to make a difference in the world. As time went by, it became easier and easier to quiet my mind in meditation.

"Then, more recently, I began to discover, in stillness and silence, a great sense of peace and bliss. Now I feel like I have become attached—almost addicted—to the bliss. I am really present when I meditate—supremely present, to use your term—but I find myself wanting to turn my back on the world and its insanity. Sometimes I feel like Nero, fiddling away while

Rome burns."

If you are serious about your spiritual quest, then having a world where everyone has the freedom to be themselves, and to express themselves creatively, has to be important to you. After all, spirituality is about awakening to wisdom and love, to the oneness we share in common with all humanity—indeed, with all life.

But as you go deeper on the path, as you learn to be more present, to relax and open up to the beauty and power of the now moment, you do feel that power in your body as bliss. With deep muscular relaxation, a flood of endorphins, the pain dissolving hormones, are released. I call endorphins "the bliss chemicals." They make you feel as if every cell in your body is vibrating with bliss, with ecstasy. It is incredibly healing and transformative. At the same time, you're opening up to the deeper, spiritual energy which infuses all creation itself. This presence is itself the source of profound harmony.

So, when this is new to you, it is understandable that you might forget about your original intention to help contribute to a freer and more loving world. It is easy to get lost in the delight of meditation, seduced by the mystery and wonder of your own travels through inner space. You begin to build a story about yourself as a seeker, as a meditator, an inner journeyer.

It happened to me. There's nothing wrong with this, for a while. Just like teenagers have to push their edges and explore their limits, so we must do the same when we are exploring our spirituality for the first time. Eventually you'll come to see even bliss has its limits. It's like sex. An orgasm would cease being enjoyable if it went on too long. Any sensation, feeling, or emotion lasting too long inevitably turns to suffering.

Bliss is a state; it comes and goes. When you get attached to a state through creating some story around it, you sow the seeds of suffering. The suffering arises either when the bliss is not there, or, the bliss *is* there, but life is calling you, and now you've got this distraction taking you away from the bliss you've grown so addicted to.

Let me tell you a story. When my son Adam was about a

year old, around the time I met Jean Klein, I reached a point in my meditations where it was easy for me to be completely present and to release all the tension in my mind and body, and open up to bliss. Waves of bliss just rolled through me, and I felt like I was in heaven. I fabricated a story around my new experience, convinced I had found enlightenment—not a hundred percent convinced, but maybe eighty or ninety.

Then, one morning as I sat to meditate, I was just beginning to cruise on the feeling of bliss, when Adam started crying from the bedroom next door. His mother Barbara called out to me, "Jim, please go change Adam's diapers. I'm busy!" I remember cringing inside. The feeling of bliss was getting really strong, and the last thing I wanted to do was get up from my meditation and change my son's soiled diapers.

Then I heard a voice inside me—the voice of my conscience, no doubt!—saying: "Jim, your son is uncomfortable, he needs his diapers changed, and you don't want to go do it because it will interrupt your blissful meditation. And you call this *enlightenment*?"

So, I got up and changed his diapers, and received a great lesson as well, a lesson now reinforced by my experience with having met Jean. Awakening, or enlightenment, as he said, is not about being attached to states of bliss, nor to states of peace, joy, stillness, or anything else.

It is about seeing through the illusion of the "me." It is about getting free of identification with thought, with the world between our ears. It is about living in awareness, being supremely present, welcoming whatever is arising, and doing what needs to be done. Whether it is changing diapers, or going to the office every day. Whether it is looking at ways to clean up the environment, help the homeless, eliminate poverty, or solving any of the other countless problems facing us as human beings.

Sooner or later you come to realize you're not on this path of freedom or spiritual awakening just for your own benefit. You're not doing it just for your own peace of mind, or to free yourself from your own conflict and stress—although it's an important first step, and is where most of us begin. Ultimately you're doing it so the world can be a better place.

More and more, the liberation from fear, the awakening of the heart, becomes your guiding vision, your *raison d'être*. Then, as your freedom, fearlessness, and compassion deepen, you'll touch people in ways you cannot even imagine.

You'll understand what Oliver Wendell Holmes meant when he said: "The place for a man who is complete in all his parts is in the fight."

You may not do great things, you may not work on a very big scale, or play in a big arena—very few of us will—but even to help your neighbor, to do good work in your own family or community, will be plenty. If each of us picked up our own garbage, spoke with kindness, and acted out of a genuine sense of respect and regard for our fellow human beings, even though we may not agree with their beliefs or condone their behavior, the world would soon change.

In any case, the delightful discovery is that when you release the attachment to bliss, you realize that bliss is always here. You just have to stop, get still, breathe, relax your body, and—presto!—peace, stillness, the bliss and fullness of *being*, it is right here. It has always been right here. It really is your true nature. It is *our* true nature...

See if you can experience it right now... Pause, and be very still, very alert, supremely present... Let go of any thoughts, and stories in your mind, and just be right here, now... *Then tune in to the vastness within, the vastness which is at the same time full... See if you can feel that fullness as bliss bubbling throughout every dimension of your being... Breathe and relax into it... Then let the idea, the story of "bliss" go, open your eyes, and just be here...*

Seeing From The Reality Behind Reality

The 8th century's Shankara, from India, was one of the original masters of nondual wisdom, the understanding of reality as fundamentally one, indivisible Whole. He said: "The realization of truth is brought about by perception, and not in the least by ten millions of acts."

What he meant by this is that all the spiritual techniques and practices, and all the good works in the world, will not set you free. Working with the body or engaging in breathing techniques won't do it. Meditation won't do it. Compassionate service to mankind won't do it. These practices are beneficial—and compassion, certainly, is needed throughout the world—but only the shift in perception I have been talking about will actually set you free: the shift from the limited, ego-bound perspective of "me, myself, and my story" into the expanded vision of clear, thought-free, present-time awareness.

The more aware of this you become, the more you intuitively realize you are not your body, mind, or senses because these can be observed. Rather, you are what is *observing*. What you actually are is pristine awareness or consciousness expressing through this unique instrument, this individual body/mind/self called "you." You are the timeless, unchanging awareness noticing and responding to the endlessly changing drama that is life. You are the consciousness giving birth to the entire world between your ears, the world that you have always thought of as "you."

The deeper the realization of yourself as the consciousness behind everything—as the ocean, expressing itself as the wave called "you"—the closer you draw to the perceptual shift that is true inner freedom.

Eventually, if you keep seeking the core truth about who you are, the realization becomes complete and you no longer have to "work" at being aware. You will see that the world between your ears really is a kind of dream-world, a self-generated fiction, a story of your own making, and just through seeing this, it begins to fall away. You don't even have to actively drop it. Once you see the story you have been so attached to is not real, you will lose interest in it, in the same way a child lets go of the Santa Claus myth (albeit with much reluctance!) upon being told Santa is not real.

Your mind no longer controls you. Instead, you as consciousness are now fully in control of it. You still have thoughts, but you now know you are not your thoughts. You still have a story, but you now know you are not your story. You still have an ego, but now you know you are not your ego. From this place of inner freedom you can then begin to use thought in a conscious, highly-intentional way. You can use the creative power of thoughts to manifest the results you seek in your life. This is what it means to see, and to live, from the Reality behind reality

As the teaching and the practice start to become more and more your way of life, your physical, mental, and emotional energies find their natural balance and harmony. Healing can then take place, often at very deep levels. If an illness or physical condition persists, it is much easier to live with and manage. Once you have awakened to your true nature, these kinds of things no longer get you down in the way they did before.

Whether it is a health problem or some other challenging or difficult circumstance, you do everything you can to address it, to heal it, to fix it, to change it, but you don't suffer because of it. If nothing can be done for the present, then you relax and accept it. You flow with it. You pay attention to the lessons to be learned, if any. You apply the learning in whatever way is appropriate.

The Teaching And Practice In Real Life

A young woman asked me: "For a long time I have been interested in spiritual matters, especially in the freedom you are speaking about. My husband doesn't support my interest. He thinks meditation and the pursuit of the spiritual life is a waste of time, just an escape, and having little to do with real life.

What do you say to this?"

I told her I was reminded of a cartoon I saw once about a young seeker who has just climbed to a mountaintop refuge, where a wise-looking, gray-bearded man is sitting on a mat. The seeker says to him, "Master, tell me please, what is the meaning of life?" The guy looks at him with his eyebrows raised, and says: "Beats me. I'm just up here hiding from my creditors."

No doubt about it, meditation and spiritual practices can be an escape from everyday life and responsibility. But as long as spirituality is taken up with the right attitude, it always brings us more fully into life. It helps us become more present because it gradually frees us from the identification with our ego and from the kinds of personal motives and agendas getting in the way of real, heartfelt communication.

Look at the current state of real life. The world is still in upheaval, with terrorist acts and clashes between warring factions ever on the rise. All wars cause an enormous amount of suffering, most of it inflicted on innocents—what the American military likes euphemistically to call "collateral damage." Regardless of who initiates the war, or who is at fault, most wars are fueled by issues of money, power, greed, and the stories people hold onto and are identified with around those issues.

Some wars are the result of ethnic, tribal, and religious conflicts, but ultimately they too are symptomatic of a deeper drive, the lust for both economic and political power. In turn, this lust for power comes out of a deep insecurity, the ego's story around what it is convinced it needs for its own survival.

Sincere seekers, like the young woman above, sometimes say to me that when they look at the world situation, it always seems so hopeless. It makes them want to escape, to seek refuge in a monastery or an ashram somewhere.

I tell them that while retreat time in monasteries or ashrams is always beneficial, any illumination we find there must be brought into the world. We must bring it from the mountaintop into the marketplace, otherwise what good is it?

When you really look at what is going on in politics and business, it is not so hard to figure out. In all countries, in all cities and towns, you have groups of men—for it is mostly men— who scheme, manipulate, and use force or violence to further their own personal interests. Meanwhile, inside themselves they live in darkness. They have become disconnected from the light of truth they once knew when they were very young. Now, they only know reflected light, the light of bright, shiny, expensive objects, or of religious artifacts, "holy" books, and creeds invested with arbitrary meaning.

They are convinced the "truth" lies in such objects, and they can only find happiness through them. Thus they live in illusion, in their story. As a result of being identified with their own dark story, they suffer tremendous anxiety and fear deep in their psyches. Through their willful and malicious actions, they inflict extraordinary amounts of suffering on innocent men, women, and children.

Awakening to inner freedom is the only way out of illusion. Awakening frees you from the ego's grip and its endless fears and insecurities. It brings you to the joy of your true nature, the joy not dependent on objects or reflected light, but the light shining from within you, the light which you *are*. This is the light Jesus spoke of when he said, "I am the Light."

It is important to remember that awakening is not just about your own bliss and freedom. The deeper you move into the enlightened awareness of your real nature, the more you feel your connection with the rest of humanity.

Then your motive for awakening becomes less personal, and more about the larger picture. You realize the sooner a critical mass of us wakes up to our true, divine nature, the sooner we'll have a world working for everyone and everything. If you have children, people, pets, or things you love then having a world which is a safe, nurturing, and harmonious environment for all of us becomes a real priority.

The teaching and practice are powerful tools to bring you into the place where wisdom and love meet, where mind and heart become one. As more of us find this union within ourselves, then regardless of whether we live in relative anonymity, or hold positions of leadership and influence, there is a cumulative effect.

The social atmosphere starts to become saturated with consciousness, and others, still not quite awake, pick up on it. It's beautiful how it works.

Helping People Get Free Of Their Stories

When I do a workshop or a private session, I am simply present with people as I guide them into the experience of being present with themselves and their environment. Sometimes, this process involves uncovering and facing the demons they haven't been willing to look at. If that is the case, I journey with them through the dark depths, and sometimes the raging inferno, of their own inner turmoil.

I guide the person through the practice—which, as you may be beginning to realize, is exquisitely simple yet powerfully transforming. As the person enters ever more deeply into the *now*, they find themselves freer of attachment to any story and the suffering it causes. They are clearer, more relaxed, more rooted in their own authentic being. Meanwhile, if it is in a workshop, the rest of the group, facing the issue they want to explore, is following along, experiencing their own little—and sometimes big—"Ah-ha" moment.

The traumatic incident from the past is typically something which happened when they were very young—being left alone by their mother on the first day of school, perhaps, and not feeling safe. Or maybe it is a memory of abandonment, sadness, guilt, or betrayal. That long ago event has been running their lives, from the shadows, ever since. I accompany them from a place of being very present. I am alert, calm, and relaxed. This encourages them to be the same. They get to explore their own past from the clear perspective of the present.

At one workshop, I worked with a middle-aged woman named Jane. Her "story" was that she was grieving the death of her Dad, who had died just two months previously. He was mostly very mean to her throughout her life, as were her two brothers, who of course had learned their behavior from their father. Nevertheless, she wanted to be with him while he was dying. She said she wanted to show him unconditional love.

She was sobbing as she was telling this story. I just listened, and was very present with her. Then she said his last act, as he was lying on his deathbed, was to touch her with surprising tenderness on the cheek, and say to her that he loved her.

A few other people in the workshop were weeping, too. As she finished telling her story, I gently directed her back to being present in this moment now. I encouraged her to be aware of her breathing, to feel the aliveness in her body, to notice her environment, the presence of the other participants in the workshop, the sound of my voice... Soon, she was deeply relaxed, and much more present. She was quite radiant, in fact, and looked at least ten years younger.

Then, about five days later, I received this email from her: "I can't tell you how different I feel. I feel like my life is changing... I feel such an amazing shift that it's hard to explain, but then I don't need to explain it to you."

She didn't need to explain it to me, because that is why I do the work I do. When people release their stories of the past, and the pent-up emotions around them, they are liberated in the present. They feel relaxed, alive, and always look younger than they did before.

Sophia was another woman I worked with privately. She was thirty-five years old and had been on a spiritual journey all her adult life. She had lived in an ashram and studied with many different teachers, yet still had not found freedom from the emotional pain of her childhood.

Her "story" was a familiar one, a story of abandonment which she had tried to heal, unsuccessfully, through her years of "spiritual" seeking. Hers was a classic case of "spiritual by-pass," using spirituality to deny, avoid, or try to "transcend" difficult and painful emotions.

When she was a child, her mother ignored her emotional needs, and her father was always busy with his work and was never around. Now, she fluctuated between experiences of real peace and bliss borne from her years of spiritual practice, and times of extreme pain, sadness, and emotional trauma, such that she found herself feeling so alone, so lost, that she didn't want to live anymore.

When I met her, she was caught in the pain of her abandonment. She was wracked with grief, sobbing like a child. I looked into her eyes and encouraged her to honor her feelings, but not go into her usual story about them, which basically was: *I feel so alone... life is not worth living... I just want to die...*

Then I said, gently but firmly: "You can handle this, Sophia. These feelings are from your childhood, but you are now thirty-five years old. You are a grown woman, wise and powerful, and you are bigger than anything you are experiencing, including these feelings and emotions. So, *be* the wise, powerful woman you are..."

Soon, she stopped crying and began to breathe more calmly and evenly. She looked back at me with a steady, open-eyed gaze. Her dark-brown eyes sparkled. Slowly, she smiled, and said, "I *can* handle it... It's true; I am bigger than the emotional pain I experience. Wow... "

Then she gave me a warm embrace, and thanked me. I said to her, "No, thank *you*. Thank you for being vulnerable enough to share your pain with me. Now you have a new *mantra* to say to yourself whenever those feelings of abandonment, and the stories around it, start to surface."

She smiled again, and said, "Yes... I can handle it."

Now, maybe the emotion being triggered is a fear of something in the future. So, I invite the person to really look at the worst-case scenario, to play it out, visualize it actually happening, but again, always from the perspective of the *present.*

When seen from the present, you realize you are always okay in this moment. The stories and worst-case scenarios appearing between your ears are just imagined, made-up, although the feelings and sensations they evoke are real. But the minute you get that you are okay *now*—which is the essence of awakening, or self-realization—the stories dissolve, and the fear and other disturbing reactions fall away.

You can do it yourself. Maybe it has to do with nervousness. Sit with the question, "What is the cause of my nervousness?" suspended in your mind. Look at it from different angles. Notice what images, memories, or thoughts may surface. Perhaps you will remember a time when you first asked a question, and the teacher scolded you or humiliated you.

You may need to probe into your past to find the emotional trauma or event, the origin of the story. Seeing the truth behind your old reactive patterns is the beginning of freedom. It takes courage to face yourself in this way. It takes trust in the process, trusting that what you get is going to be better than what you are letting go of. You don't know that going in. In a way, you have to free fall.

When you face the trauma, there may be emotion, the experiencing of an old wound. You may get angry, sad, depressed. You have to be present with it. You have to learn to welcome whatever is there.

Once, in a workshop, a man had a memory spontaneously surface. He told me: "I remember this very crabby teacher from second grade, jabbing her finger at me and telling me if I had been paying attention like all the other boys and girls, I wouldn't need to ask such a stupid question. So, what do I do with this memory?"

I answered him by saying that there are many ways of addressing this, or any other problem. The decision of how to approach it is always yours. I teach the direct way, the direct path. When the forgotten memory—and the story around it—surfaces, and you realize that this is indeed where the nervousness or fear originated, simply hold it in your consciousness. Hold the past scene in your awareness. Remember all the details you can. See it vividly. Keep breathing as you do this.

If it brings up emotion and starts to get too intense, you can always let it go and come back to it later, maybe when you meditate tomorrow morning. Just make sure you come back to it, and quickly. You want to deal with this and be done with it. Our goal is to let go and release whatever gets in the way of our being here, fully present and available to life in this moment.

Basically, you just face the old wound and the story around it from this very clear, centered, grounded awareness. Welcome it. After all, it is showing you where you are not yet free.

You may notice that because you are able to observe this scene dispassionately in your mind, the memory of the scene is *not* who you are. Who you really are is what is looking or observing, which is pure, unbounded awareness, or consciousness itself. This is the shift in perception I have spoken of. The more you stand firm in this place of present-time awareness, the less charge and emotional reactivity the memory will generate.

When you shine the light of intense, present-time awareness on a story, thought, sensation, or feeling, what you are observing undergoes a change. Stories, thoughts, and pictures in the mind dissolve, uncomfortable sensations and feelings in the body unwind, and a feeling of true clarity and harmony begins to unfold throughout your entire being.

A Practice For Being Present

*Whenever upset, anxiety, or suffering arises, **be present with it**, even welcome it. Ask yourself: "What am I experiencing right now?" Pay attention to the feelings and sensations of the contraction or disturbance.*

*Then **notice the story** you are telling yourself, whatever the story is. If you like, you can step back with your awareness, out of the story. This helps you see it more clearly. If necessary, play out the worst-case scenario.*

*Then **see the truth**. See that you are the one who sees. Take a deep, slow breath, and relax. Be very alert with your whole being. Continue to notice the sensations in your body. Feel the* *energy, the aliveness in your cells. Listen to the sounds around you. Look at the things, natural and human-made, in your environment.*

Now see the connection between the story and the upset emotion in your body. Allow the emotion, which is real in this moment, to be there, but don't go into your head, don't go into any new stories or thoughts about it. Just be the spacious, present-time awareness you are, looking out through your eyes at the whole of life. Be the unchanging awareness behind the ever-changing stories, behind the ever-changing emotions.

Do this practice and, I promise you, your energy will soon shift. So long as you continue to be very alert and aware, and don't go into concepts, into denial or rejection of the emotion, into analyzing or trying to understand, or anything else, the contracted emotion will unwind, dissolve. You will feel more relaxed, more at ease, more present.

Then you will find that while you still have thoughts and feelings, "you," as the awareness or consciousness which watches and experiences everything, will be senior to them. Your thoughts will not be a problem. They will have no emotional charge. Then you can use thinking for the powerful, creative tool it is.

You can use it to manifest whatever your heart desires. That's its job. You can think of it as the "right use of thought."

Chapter Four

Questioning This "Me"

Once you become accustomed to being present with whatever is happening, and looking for the story behind your times of conflict, upset, or suffering, you will inevitably begin—if you are at all curious—to question the very "me" you think you are. This is where you take the fourth step I spoke about at the end of the Introduction.

With deep self-inquiry, you'll see that the "me" is just a story too—the root of all stories, the story-*teller*—and that your true nature is the lucid, unchanging consciousness behind everything.

It is about looking into the very heart of who and what you take yourself to be. You have to understand, not just at an intellectual level, but with every fiber of your being, who you really are and what your place in the cosmos is. Paradoxically, you arrive at this understanding by observing and discovering who and what you are *not*.

It is seeing and understanding you are not your body, mind, story, thoughts, or senses. You cannot be them, in the most essential sense, because you are observing them. What you are is the consciousness aware of them, *seeing* them. Your true nature, in other words, *is* consciousness itself.

The practice we have been cultivating prepares you for

this understanding. The teaching *is* the understanding. It is the simple yet elegant explanation of the true nature of reality, the metaphysical framework which informs and brings light to your mind, and points it in the right direction, back within, where truth lies.

There are two aspects to the teaching: the primary aspect and the secondary aspect. The primary aspect explores the principal barrier to presence, which is thinking. This exploration leads you to the realization you are not your thoughts, not your story, but rather you are the awareness or consciousness behind the thoughts. This is the discovery that frees you from your mind and leads to liberation.

The secondary aspect has to do with conscious creation, with the conscious use of thought and intention to create the reality you desire. When we understand thoughts have power, we can then use thinking in a conscious way, from a very clear-headed space. This is where awakening to inner mastery leads naturally to outer mastery, to success in the world of the marketplace.

Once you understand the teaching, know it at the core of your being, deep enough to produce the shift in perception which sets you free, you won't need to keep it at the forefront of your mind any more. You won't need to contemplate it. It will have done its job. Once in a while, if some residue of self-doubt appears, you have the teaching—"I am not this story, I am the awareness *behind* the story"—to remind you of what is real. And the teaching is there to share with others who are still seeking, and want to know what must happen if they are to be free.

The practice, however, is what you *do*, and is available as long as you need it. It is a practice for both finding freedom, and for living itself. Residues from old patterns, from your story, can still arise when you are tired or sick, and you may have to make an effort to be present. Occasionally, during the first few years after awakening, old tendencies to resist or refuse something in your inner experience may also occur, but you will have these tools to gently remind yourself to be vulnerable, to accept what is, and to embrace it all.

Through the practice of presence you embody the teaching and the understanding which has been revealed to you. This practice enables you to translate what you learn from meditation into the reality of the marketplace of daily life; it brings you into your heart and opens you to unconditional love. Once you are fully awake, then you are always present.

To understand the teaching, it helps to look again at the nature of suffering and how it arises. Suffering, in the way I define it, is the mental and emotional distress resulting from feeling victimized by some situation or circumstance in one's life.

Something happens, whether real or imagined—pain, illness, unexpected change, loss, a setback, or a difficult situation—and it provokes a reaction. It pushes a button, and you don't like it. You don't like what is happening. You already have a story around the event, and you create an even bigger, more dramatic story, which in turn, increases stress and upset. As a result, you are discontented, unhappy, even more miserable. This is what it means to suffer.

Someone once asked me: "In what way is suffering different than just feeling your emotions? Isn't grieving the death of a loved one a kind of suffering too?"

Suffering is different from feeling your emotions deeply. Grieving the loss of someone you love, or feeling angry at the injustice in the world, at seeing someone harm another, is natural and normal. It is not suffering. When your heart is open to life, when you live in a state of acceptance, or welcoming, you feel these things very deeply, and the feelings last as long as they last.

Some people may feel deep, intense grief at the loss of a loved one for a week or a month and then it is basically over, except for residual waves of emotion which may continue to wash over them from time-to-time. Others, perhaps because the bond with the loved one was so strong, may be in mourning for much longer. They need to take their time letting go. It is their way of honoring the remarkable connection, the story they shared with the person they loved, who is now gone. Again, this is not necessarily suffering.

Suffering is when you don't *like* what you are feeling or what is happening, and it makes you unhappy. It is always due to some form of resistance, which causes you to close down in some fashion. It is the exact opposite of being open, welcoming, and vulnerable. Conflict, self-doubt, anxiety, guilt, resentment, fear, loneliness, depression, and all other forms of discontent and unhappiness are always the result of resisting what is.

Resistance, in turn, is caused by holding onto beliefs, judgments, expectations, and pictures about the way things are or should be. It comes from fabricating, in your mind, some kind of story about what is happening. For example, you feel a numbing, tired sensation in your body, and you say to yourself: "I don't like this, I must be depressed." Or you notice someone look at you in a strange way. You think you are being judged and start to feel guilty or angry.

You can let go of the thoughts that are the source of the resistance, the story, and simply be present with what is. When you breathe into and flow with the ever-changing moods, feelings, and circumstances you will no longer experience conflict or suffering. However, letting go of resistance to what is—of your assumptions, expectations, judgments, and so on— is not always easy. It is relatively easy for most people to let go of their inner agenda in some circumstances, but they find it very difficult in highly personal situations with an intense emotional charge.

To let go of resistance at the deepest level, so you can be fully open to life and other people in each moment—which is one of the signs of awakening—you must explore the very source of resistance itself. You must examine the ego, the personal "I," the "one" inside you who is suffering. From the perspective of consciousness, your wholeness, you must look at this "me" who attaches meaning and importance to the story.

Another way of viewing this is to contemplate the notion that we are not our thoughts or our story, but rather we are the consciousness giving birth to it all. I call this the global or holistic approach. In Sanskrit, it is the *jnana* path to truth.

It may also be termed the wisdom or discernment path to enlightenment. You orient the mind towards clarity. Give it a perspective or belief which is relatively true. It is true because experiencing it radically transforms how you see reality. With this comprehension, you eventually realize what was previously only a belief for you is actually the way it really is.

You have literally stepped, or "popped" outside the "self" which, a moment ago, you believed that you were, and now you are viewing life from the perspective of the Whole. You have awakened to full consciousness. You know yourself *as* consciousness, and what this feels like is unlimited spaciousness, boundlessness, openness. It is love. There is no separation, only total connection to everything which is, ever was, and ever will be.

Speaking personally, there is no real difference between in here, inside my head, and out there, in the world. There is no "me" feeling separate, no center and no border. There is just the flow of the universe, of life, and I, as consciousness, am one with it.

Consequently, I find myself open to all people and to all experiences. This is the essence or ground of unconditional love. I may not like the behavior of certain people, and may speak out against it or even reject it, but I am at least open to it. I may not like certain experiences, but I have learned the wisdom of not arguing with reality, of not struggling with what *is*. Thus, I live in peace and serenity.

Once you have awakened, while things may go on outwardly pretty much as they did before, your inner life is never the same again. At the same time, there will undoubtedly be some outward changes. You will approach life much more consciously.

Find Out Who Wants To Be Free

Meditation, as you know by now, brings clarity to the mind. Watching the breath, feeling the sensations move through the body, and witnessing the flow of thoughts and pictures as they move through the mind trains your power of attention. Meditation brings you to a place of inner tranquility enabling you to see reality more clearly.

I meditated a lot during my time as a seeker. When I sat I would watch my own mind and emotional reactions constantly, and pursuing my own line of self-inquiry as I struggled inwardly to free myself of everything binding me.

Along the way, I formed a friendship with two men who became my *dharma*-buddies, or allies on the spiritual path— Erich Schiffmann and Darrell Price. The unique aspect of our relationship was its focus: all three of us wanted enlightenment, inner freedom, more than anything else. We spent a lot of time hanging out together, doing yoga, meditating in silence, and going for long hikes in nature. Above all, we found ourselves engaging in an ongoing, spirited dialogue around such subjects as the teachings of Krishnamurti, Ramana Maharshi, Zen, *A Course in Miracles*, and our own driving quest for freedom.

As serious as we were about awakening, we were still able to laugh at ourselves. In fact, we called our one-track conversation "the endless yarn." We used to wonder which of us was going to, as we put it, "go over the top" first. Those were heady times as we contemplated the vast spiritual possibilities before us!

Like many seekers, I had a number of other illuminating experiences and other breakthroughs during my years on the path, beginning with my very first taste of oneness that summer's morning. I was definitely a lot freer inwardly, more relaxed, more present. I still mostly believed in the possibility of inner freedom, in the reality of awakening. But sometimes I wondered.

Sometimes I questioned whether there really was a "top" to go over, and if this life of continuing meditation and inquiry, with its times of great peace and beauty, punctuated by periods of conflict and self-doubt, was as good as it was going to get.

Of course, as I found out, meditation alone won't set you free. If you want true freedom, you have to sit with the question: "*Who* is meditating?"

Once you have learned to easily shift states of stress and

tension by doing the practice, then you have to look within and find the meditator. Find out where the urge to meditate, to seek refuge or peace, truly springs from. Discover who and what you are, who this "person" meditating really is. There is a Zen story that speaks to this.

The old master noticed his most eager student sitting hours and hours in meditation, way longer than any of the other practitioners who came to the *zendo* to meditate. He went up to him late one morning after all the others had left to go and prepare for lunch.

"What are you doing?" the master asked.

Without breaking his concentration, without even opening his eyes, the student replied: "I am meditating to get enlightened."

"Ah, so," said the master. He picked up a stone and a brick tile, sat down near the student, and began rubbing away at the tile with the stone. He made quite a noise, even huffing and puffing a little as he worked.

An hour passed, and when the student couldn't stand it anymore, he turned, opened his eyes, and inquired, "Master, can you please tell me what *you* are doing?"

"I am polishing this brick tile to make a mirror," the master responded, without interrupting his work.

The student's eyes widened. "But it's not possible. Nobody could make a mirror out of a brick tile."

"Just so," said the master, as he put the rock and tile down. He looked intently at the student. "And nobody ever got enlightened just by sitting and meditating."

What this story says to me is once we are able to access the relaxed, clear presence meditation brings, we then have to look within. We then have to start looking at this "I" who wants freedom, who seeks meaning, who yearns for the secret of life. This is the art and practice of self-inquiry: to look deep within yourself to the very source of reality, of the "I" or "me" itself.

When you are worrying, stop and ask yourself, "*Who* is worrying?" Then dive deep within and really look. Find out where the "I" who says it's worrying comes from. When you are feeling bored or restless, ask yourself "*Who* is bored? *Who* is restless?*" Go within, and look for the source, the location of this "I" who insists it is bored. When you are suffering, when you are feeling a little blue or lonely, breathe consciously and ask yourself, "So, *who* is feeling lonely?" Then look inside. Seek the origin of the "I" thought.

Really stop and probe within, beyond the thought forms "I feel this" or "I feel that." Look beyond the story you are telling yourself about your suffering. Listen to the silence behind the thoughts. Feel yourself at the most essential level of your being *as* awareness, pure consciousness, the source, expressing through this body/mind/self called you. Find out who you are.

As you discover who this "I" is and from whence it arises, a day will come when you'll see it is not real. It is only a concept, an idea, albeit an extremely deep-rooted one. Then fear will leave you and love will become the dominant reality in your heart. Find out who wants to be free, and you'll no longer feel bound...

Pause right now... Take a deep breath, relax, and be very still, supremely alert, fully present... Now go within and see if you, as the awareness present, the pure consciousness which is aware of being here, can find this "I" you have taken yourself to be all these years... Can you find it anywhere within, other than as a fleeting ghost? Can you find any concept or thought? If you probe to the very core of your being, you'll come up empty-handed... There is nothing there, no-thing, except your awareness, the awareness looking at everything within and without... So, look at the beauty within and around you, and be the awareness you are...

Breaking Through The Story Of "Me"

In 1983, my seeking and restlessness grew to the point where I knew I had to sell my practice and go to India. Other Western seekers had gone there and, if they hadn't found complete enlightenment, had at least deepened their spiritual experience.

At this point I was very successful materially—which was what allowed me to take nine months off to travel, and pay all the expenses for my new girlfriend, Barbara, and me. I was making a lot of money seeing patients just three days a week, owned a four-bedroom house with an in-ground pool, drove a brand new BMW, and had no debt other than the house. Several of my friends thought I was crazy to give it all up, but you have to understand the mind-set of the true spiritual seeker, which I was: nothing else matters, least of all material success, as long as the Holy Grail of enlightenment, of inner freedom, is still being sought.

We traveled to China, Bali, Nepal, India, Australia, and back to New Zealand. I can sum up my experience of the journey in a few words: heat, dust, a sea of people, noise, cheap hotels, the thrill of strange and exotic sights, a lot of disillusion, and the glimmerings of an awakening to something new.

When we arrived back in California in 1984, Barbara got pregnant, we married, I started a small practice again, and at the end of that year I met the man who was to be my teacher or guide on the path of enlightenment, Jean Klein. At the time, he was in his seventies, and his influence on me turned out to be profound.

I remember I really wanted the inner freedom Jean spoke about. I wanted it with all my heart, but I was often hesitant to ask him questions. I felt a little intimidated by his rather detached, austere, somewhat forbidding old-world European demeanor. Nevertheless, I'd eventually take a deep breath, muster up my courage, and put forth the question that was on my mind. Sometimes though, the questions arose spontaneously.

Once, without any forethought, I found myself asking him:

"Do you ever experience fear?"

He looked at me for what seemed to be minutes (Jean lived in inner silence, and always took a long time to respond to questions). Then he said, with a smile, "Who is there to be afraid?"

I sat contemplating his answer. It was the essence of the whole teaching: when you don't take yourself to be anybody, when you're not holding on to any image or concept of "self," there is nothing in you to resist the flow of life, to be in conflict with whatever is happening. There is nothing in you worrying about the future, or what may happen in the next moment, and so there is no fear. This is what it means to be free.

In order to fully realize the freedom that is your true nature, you have to turn inward and find out who and what is doing the looking. You have to find the looker. You have to be a fearless warrior to advance on this, the final leg of the journey. You have to really look deeply within, and face yourself with rigorous honesty. But the rewards are there, awaiting your discovery, because this is the stage when consciousness fully evolves, becomes completely awakened within us.

In Zen it is said of this final stage: "Mountains are once again mountains, and rivers are once again rivers."

Now, however, the mountains shine with a radiance that could not be perceived before, and the rivers seem to flow right through us, cleansing our very souls. Moreover, it is always thus, for when we awaken to our true nature, everything, everyday, seems fresh and new. The mountains, we realize, are no different in their essence than we are. They, like us, are expressions of the one universal energy, or consciousness, that is the source of all creation.

As we have seen, the beginning stages of the spiritual journey are addressed by religion, mythic stories, and belief systems. The intermediate stages are about spirituality itself, the direct and personal experience of what religion is talking about. The final phase is characterized by realization, by awakening to inner freedom.

True inner freedom is the fulfillment of the religious promise held out to us as we first set out on our journey. Religion, through its many stories and beliefs around personal redemption and salvation, has given way to this new freedom: the jewel of deep spiritual wisdom, of clear insight into the true nature of reality.

With this ultimate freedom, concepts, beliefs, and questions fall away. We let go of the identification with the personal "story" which had previously given—or seemed to have given—such meaning to our lives. We let go of it because we see it isn't even real: it is just a fiction of our own making.

Whatever our particular story was, the fact is we made it up. We based it on all our past experiences, whether actual or imagined, and then added a smorgasbord of beliefs, opinions, and value judgments about what we thought we needed to do to survive. Yet once we see it is just a story, why would we want to persist in "believing" it? Why would any intelligent person cling to what is unreal?

By the time we get to this point in our evolution, we are ready to understand and embody the teaching. With the teaching it becomes clear that to hold onto any concept or story prevents us from a deeper experience of truth in the now. But to get free of the holding, we have to explore how it comes about in the first place.

Thus, the primary spiritual practice at this stage is self-inquiry, or asking: "Who am I?" "Who is it that wants to believe?" "Who is it that worries?" and "Who is it that suffers?"

This is the technique known as *vichara*, self-inquiry, given to us by the great nondual sage Ramana Maharshi, from southern India. Through self-inquiry, and with the understanding that we are no longer going to settle for any conceptual answers, we dive directly into the source of the mind, the ego, and the "me."

As self-inquiry deepens, what we have already perceived in glimpses starts to become stunningly clear: we have thoughts, even the thought "I" or "me," but we cannot be our thoughts. We are, instead, whatever is observing them. And what is that? Consciousness, or awareness, itself. All thoughts, sensations, and forms arise within the context of the pure, formless consciousness we are.

No matter what we are thinking or experiencing, what we fundamentally are is the awareness behind the thought, sensation, or feeling. Our true nature is pure awareness, or consciousness, expressing through our body, mind, and personality.

Breathing happens; sensations, feelings, and emotions come and go; thoughts pass through the mind; and stories about our experience form, but the only continuous, unbroken, and always present "thing" is consciousness itself. Consciousness is that which, in us, is *aware* of all these changing phenomena. This is the nondual truth of existence...

So, relax into your true nature... Be present
as the beautiful, shining awareness you are...
Notice the flow of your breath, the sensations
in your body, any feelings and emotions arising,
the thoughts and stories in your mind, including
the "I" or "me" thought... Notice whatever
happens to be in your physical surroundings...
Notice how you are the awareness which is
aware of all these arising phenomena... And it
all comes and goes, appears and disappears, in
you... But you, as the awareness noticing it all,
are always here...

The more we see *from* our true nature, the more the identification with mind-based identities—to ego, and to ideas and images of "self"—falls away. Then the emotional baggage in the psyche, which is expressed in the body, starts to dissolve naturally. Our head clears, in other words, and the psychologically and emotionally generated tension and stress start to leave the body.

With the releasing of tension, we feel a tremendous sense of inner spaciousness and ease. This expansiveness allows the pure light of consciousness to enter. We come to an authentic openness, a true vulnerability, where we hold onto nothing, and allow everything to flow through us.

Eventually, we even let go of attachment to the "knowing," to the "Now I am awake!" story. We are content just to be the beautiful expression of consciousness we are. Nor need we hold onto blissful or sacred experiences because we realize, at last, that bliss and the sacred are our true nature. We simply have to breathe, relax, and be open to the present, welcoming it all.

Now there is a new feeling of lightness, an ease of being, and with it the realization of the truth of the Zen saying: "After enlightenment, nothing changes, but everything is somehow different."

Life still goes on as before. Work needs to be done and responsibilities must be met. The difference is in the awareness now shining through us. We are simply wide awake in the present. With our ego and our personal history no longer in the way, it is as if we perceive everything and every moment with new eyes.

Toss The Ego A Bone

Some spiritual teachings support the idea of getting rid of the ego, even "annihilating" it, to become enlightened or free. Yet, upon awakening, we find that the ego is still here. Indeed, in terms of conscious creation, your ego will become your ally. Conscious use of the ego enables you to will specific actions to take place or manifest certain things into being. Ken Wilber, in his book, *One Taste*, has this to say about the ego:

"The ego is not an obstruction to Spirit, but a radiant manifestation of Spirit... It remains as the functional self in the gross realm, and it might even appropriately be intensified and made more powerful, simply because it is now plugged into the entire Kosmos. Many of the great enlightened teachers had a big ego... in the sense of strong, forceful, powerful personalities."

Perhaps Freud's influence is why people in the West often

have a confused or incorrect idea of what the "ego" is. Ego can be thought of as something negative, as in, "That guy has a lot of ego," saying he is full of self-importance. Or, ego can mean an individual is very unsure of him or herself, as in, "That person has a very insecure ego." Undoubtedly, ego is equated with self-image and self-worth. Inflated self-worth can indicate arrogance and a lack of self-worth can indicate low self-esteem.

My use of the term "ego" simply refers to the personal sense of "I" or "me." Whenever you say, "I must go and call my mother," or "I have to get to work," or "I need to fix dinner," it is your ego, or your "I," speaking. In this sense, everyone has an ego. Even though you may have realized your true nature, and no longer feel separate from the timeless flow of creation, you still have an ego. You still need to be able to define your personal wants, needs, and desires, even though they may be minimal, and even though you are now no longer attached to them.

Developing a healthy ego and a clear set of boundaries at the personal level is a vital part of the growth and maturation process happening early in our life's journey. But the proof of maturation is when we begin to see the limitations of the ego. The ego can serve us in terms of our physical survival and well-being through its ability to remember, to project and plan, to analyze and reason, to intuit and create, and to define personal boundaries, but it cannot give us all we need.

The separate, stand-alone nature of the ego cannot provide us with the deeper nourishment, the feeling of love so vital to our spiritual well-being. For this, the heart must speak. And for the heart to speak and be heard, the ego must surrender its control. It must, in effect, fade into the background.

This is beautifully expressed in the wisdom of J. Krishnamurti, who said that you must die every day in order to be free.

This means letting go of all the mental and emotional attachments which make up the ego or personal self—the attachment to beliefs, expectations, and desires. And the more you see such "stories" are not real, the more they fall away. When the ego gets out of the way something new and vital is born. This something is your real self, the true "I," the *I am* in you standing on its own—clear, strong, and vibrant.

The ego needs a story, needs to identify with or call itself something: a member of this organization or that political party, a follower of this belief or that cause. The true *I*, that which you really are in your essence, needs no such label or identification in order to know itself or to feel secure. The true, pure *I* knows itself as itself, and that is enough. It knows itself to be an expression of the divine fullness of life, a fullness lacking nothing, which is one with all humanity, with all creation.

As you open up to a more relaxed and alert way of living in the present, as you become comfortable with the silence of your true nature, you have less need for the beliefs, concepts, and stories with which the ego loves to embellish itself. Then your ego, your personal "I," will assume its rightful place in the totality of your being. Like your mind, your ego is an instrument, a tool existing for a very definite purpose. It is your personal boundary-setter. It is how you, as the ocean of consciousness, define and differentiate your individual wave-ness, your own personal creative expression.

The difference is, with the awakening to freedom, your ego becomes much more functional. It becomes transparent, a clear window. It is no longer caught up in any story about who and what you are, or what is important in your life. You are able to say "I must buy groceries," or "I am going to the park," and there is no fuss, no unnecessary drama.

However, when you have not yet awakened to your true nature, your ego, your "I" or "me" always has some kind of story attached to it. Whether you say it out loud or not, you are always feeling the need to justify, defend, affirm, or get validation for your point of view, your position, and for your sense of who you are.

As your inner freedom deepens, your ego—like your hand, voice, or any tool you might use—is there when you need it. And when you don't need it, it's out of the way. It's not a problem.

And if your ego rears its head once in a while, as it is bound to—perhaps getting caught up in a moment of pride, or self-congratulation—don't worry about it too much. I remember Sunyata, a Danish man who lived much of his life in India, and who embodied an inner silence and presence which attracted many people to him, saying it was okay to toss the ego a bone once in a while. After all, it is part of who we are.

Acknowledge your ego's existence, and let it go. Come back to simply being open and aware in this moment now. Then your ego need not be a problem.

Embrace Change

In a moment of vulnerability, a young woman said to me: "Sometimes, when I think about it, I have a great fear of change. I want the people I love to continue to be in my life. I love the house I live in. I want to stay there always. Yet I realize at some level it is just the story about change, about having to let go of things, that bothers me. Nevertheless, the fear of change still comes up..."

The Buddha taught three fundamental laws, or tenets of life. The first was the law of *anicca*, or impermanence, which says everything is always changing. The seasons come and go, day turns into night, the climate changes, our body grows and matures and then, like all living things, begins eventually to wither and die. We can't stop change, and to resist it causes dissatisfaction, or suffering. This is *dukkha*, the Buddha's second law.

So, when you see the truth of this, you don't hold onto things. You don't cling to *nama* and *rupa*, which are the Sanskrit terms for the world of name and form. You don't keep insisting things be a certain way. You learn to flow with the ups and downs of life, to take action when you need to, and to wait patiently when patience is what is required.

The well-known serenity prayer evokes this way of being: "God grant me the serenity to accept the things I cannot change, the courage to change the things I can, and the wisdom to know the difference."

122

A story the Buddhist teacher, Jack Kornfield, tells about his teacher, Achaan Cha, illustrates the same point in a different way. It revolves around a beautiful glass goblet he was given as a gift. He held and admired the goblet, while telling the gathered students that the glass was already broken. When they asked what he meant, he said one day, a year from now, or ten years, or a hundred years, something would happen—an accident, a fire, or someone would just drop the goblet—and it would break.

Because of this knowing, he could fully appreciate the goblet and enjoy using it without any attachment. He had already said goodbye to it, so every day it was in his possession was a blessing.

Another, more colorful way of saying this is that "shit happens." Wisdom is seeing the big picture, seeing the inevitable unfolding of events. It's looking ahead, and—to use a very practical expression—visualizing the worst-case scenarios. Then you are prepared. If the worst-case scenario does happen, you can take action to deal with it. You don't obsess about what might happen in the future, but you remain aware of and open to the possibilities.

You honor the past without clinging to it, you keep an eye on the future without obsessing over it, but all the time your awareness is grounded right here in the present.

The Buddha's third law is the law of *anatta*, or no-self. He said the "self" we take ourselves to be doesn't exist, except as an idea or concept in the mind. This is what all the great enlightenment traditions speak about and what Jean Klein taught as well.

It is the attachment to notions of "self," to the idea of "I am this" or "I am that," to the whole inside-our-head drama called "me, myself, and my story," which creates the resistance to change. You know what I mean: the fixed positions people take and cling to for security, whether it's a religious belief, a political belief, a national identity, or something else.

Buddha's first law, *anicca* or impermanence, accurately describes everything as constantly changing. Yet we desperately try to cling to some part of it and keep it from changing. It is this clinging, this resistance (or its opposite, aversion, a pushing away of one thing while holding on to something else) which in turn results in *dukkha*, suffering.

But the real cause of suffering is the primary clinging to any idea of "self," to being "somebody," or identifying with "my" personal history. Let go of that, see it isn't even real, and you are free. Then you live without needing to cling to any concept of "self," because you have turned your attention back in on yourself and have discovered "you" don't exist, except as a concept inside your head.

Then there is no struggle with "self" esteem. You're not holding onto any image of a "self" needing validation or approval, or feeling pleased with itself on some days, and hating itself on others. Then there is no more suffering. You always feel good inside because you're in touch with the underlying goodness of life. You use the words "I," "me," and "mine" purely in a utilitarian way, just as you use thinking for the practical, creative tool it is, but you are no longer identified with thoughts or the thinker.

Carlos Castaneda's teacher, Don Juan, put it this way: "I used to have a personal history, but then, like smoking and drinking, I saw it was no longer necessary, so I dropped it."

With the direct path approach, you learn to "drop your personal history" by seeing that it isn't real. It's only a story about something that *was* true, but isn't so now. Then an enormous weight leaves you. You don't have to prove yourself to anyone. You don't have to defend yourself, because no matter what anyone says, you don't feel attacked. Every moment is fresh and new.

A man asked me once: "Is there anything which doesn't change?" I replied yes. Consciousness itself does not change. It just *is*. Consciousness, or awareness—what is sensing and perceiving in you right now—is timeless, spaceless, causeless. It is ever-present, the silent background to the ever-changing flux and flow of creation. To understand this is to walk through the door to inner freedom.

The Buddha did not really speak about consciousness being our true nature. He simply said enlightenment was the end of suffering. However, the direct path taught by Jean Klein did emphasize this aspect. We come to freedom through awakening to the changeless, timeless awareness behind all phenomena, to the fact that consciousness itself is our true nature, who and what we are.

At this point you might ask, "How can I know this for sure?" Let's take a little trip. Look back at your life, as far back as you can remember, and think about all the changes you have gone through. Think about the friends and relationships you've had and let go of, the places you once lived, the schools you attended, the jobs you've had, the beliefs you once held so dear but have long since modified or downright rejected.

Now, see if this rings true. Notice if there is one thing which hasn't changed. Notice how your *awareness* of all these changes you have gone through has had a kind of constancy to it. It's as if, since the very beginning, there is something in you which has been watching the whole drama of your life unfold, shift, and go through its changes.

Most people understand this, and they often ask if that which doesn't change is the Witness, or the Observing Self. However, I prefer to call it simply awareness, or consciousness. It is too easy to make an object out of the idea of a "Witness" or an "Observing Self," and then you are attached to another concept, another thing. This gets you back into your head and mind—into duality, into a story. When you live in duality, the seeds of conflict and suffering are sown.

It is not really your awareness or my awareness I am referring to; it is universal awareness or divine consciousness expressing through us. Remember, there is just one ocean, one energy manifesting in all these wave forms we are. There is just one consciousness here. Realize this and it will change your life forever...

*See if you can feel or sense the one
consciousness right now... Be very still and
present... Be the awareness looking out through
your open eyes... Notice everything within and
around you... Tune into the vastness within and
without... Notice how there is just one flow of
energy, of consciousness, and you are simply one
with the flow... Thoughts can come and go in
the awareness you are, but you are not identified
with them... You are just being here, breathing
with the moment....*

Don't Take Yourself To Be Anybody

Once, at a public dialogue with Jean Klein, a man raised his hand to speak. When Jean acknowledged him, the man said: "Every time I come to hear you, I notice you seem so clear and relaxed. You radiate a peaceful, loving warmth. You seem happy. Yet I am always discontented and often stressed out. There are times when I feel quite miserable. What is the difference between us?"

Jean looked at the man for a while, and then said, with a smile: "You still take yourself to be somebody. I don't take myself to be anybody."

Until we have done it enough times, letting go of the need to be somebody can cause anxiety. We get used to relying on our thoughts, beliefs, and story to give our life meaning. It becomes our sense of identity, our sense of knowing who and what we are. Yet, this very limited way of knowing keeps us in conflict. It keeps us divided from other human beings whose identities are based on different psychological, philosophical, or religious beliefs.

Early in my journey, I did not like hearing the American spiritual teacher, Ram Dass, say in order to be enlightened you had to be nobody. Since childhood, I wanted to *be* somebody, to make my mark in life. I was always ambitious, probably due to my need for recognition and attention.

Eventually, though, I discovered Ram Dass was correct. The freest people don't take themselves to be anybody. Their ambition is less personal and more focused on just doing something worthwhile, something serving the greater good. They are not attached to any concept or image of "self," because they see all such concepts and images as unreal, figments of our own creation. Non-attachment is the result of clearly seeing the true nature of reality. It frees us from worry and suffering.

Jean's strength as a teacher was in not giving any credence to the personal. People came to him with their personal problems, but he would seldom give direct answers or advice.

Instead, he guided them back to the clarity, freedom, and the vastness which was their true impersonal nature. From his perspective, once we are established in the impersonal and awake, knowing we really are "nobody," then there is room for the personal—our personality—to emerge in an authentic, spontaneous way. The beauty of this approach is it allows us to be "somebody" without being attached to the *idea* of being "somebody." This is what it means to be free.

Yet many had difficulty with Jean's style. They didn't want to let go of their personal story, their "I," their "me." They wanted quick fixes and immediate solutions, and they didn't want to have to give up anything in return, least of all their attachment to their beliefs and ideas about who they thought they were. They came to hear Jean speak thinking they wanted freedom, when all they really wanted was a bigger prison inside which their ego could roam around.

If you want real freedom it is very important to understand this. If the sometimes impersonal nature of the direct-path teachings triggers anxiety in you, it is just an indication of the degree of identification with your ego and your personal history. Letting go of your ideas about who you are can be unsettling, even scary, yet only when you let go, can true freedom—and joy—be found. The letting go is made easier when you see that what you are identified with is not even real.

Meister Eckhart once said the less there is of "I," the more there is of God. He was referring to getting our ego out of the way. The ego, the "me," is what gets in the way of anything new happening. Still, we need an ego to survive in the world. It is part of who and what we are. It is an instrument of the body/mind/self.

Doing the three-step practice will help you to embody the teaching: you are not your thoughts or story. Gradually, the attachment to notions of "I, "me," and "mine" will loosen. You will start losing interest in this "self" you once attached such great importance to. You will see that clinging creates resistance to what is. Clinging is holding onto or believing in judgments, expectations, and attachment to outcomes. This resistance results in conflict, self-doubt, worry, fear, and suffering.

Instead of needing to hold onto any idea or image of "self," you will live in openness and awareness in the present. You won't be attached to the past, nor will you be obsessing about the future. The deeper energy of creation itself will feed you, unfolding as an incredible dynamism each time you get still and tune in to the energy of now.

You will be free. Other people's approval will not matter to you and their disapproval will have little or no effect. You will still have an ego, but it will be transparent. It will be a clear window through which your true wisdom, beauty, and essence will shine.

When you start to awaken, the ego has a tendency to keep sneaking in through the back door. With a sense of accomplishment and pride, it can say things like, "Hey, I'm enlightened," "I have arrived," or "I'm special." This is referred to as spiritual arrogance. But, as long as your awakening is genuine, you will quickly notice this and ease right back into presence. You have the skills to successfully get your ego to back off and mind its own business. You will be more interested in meeting people at a heart level, rather than from the head.

A Native American elder once said knowledge divides the world and wisdom makes it whole. Knowledge is mainly of the head, but wisdom is very much of the heart. Listen to and trust your heart, and every step of your journey will be guided by wisdom.

My Realization

The first awakening I experienced with Jean was at a retreat at Mount Madonna Center, in the Santa Cruz Mountains of California, a few years after meeting him. I was walking down to the afternoon dialogue, contemplating the notion of not being the "person" I'd taken myself to be, when my "I," my ego—with its whole story-line—suddenly jumped out into my awareness.

In an instant, I saw the game I'd been playing. I saw my attachment to the identity of myself as a spiritual "seeker," and how much juice and meaning the "seeker" identity gave me for so many years. However, the attachment to being a seeker is as much a barrier to freedom as is the attachment to any other identity.

When I saw this about myself, I felt a great sadness. I knew I needed to let it go, and I sensed at a very deep level I would never be able to quite buy into my own "story" again. I told Jean what happened.

He said: "You have, in a certain way, understood that the existence of the person is an illusion, a fabrication from memory... Live completely in the absence of yourself, and you'll become a happy man."

Gradually, I felt myself getting freer of the mind's chatter. I was more awake, more open and present, more *here*.

Two events that occurred a couple of years before my final awakening were significant in my "story." The first was a broken heart I experienced when a love affair with a much younger woman ended soon after I turned forty-six. My "enlightenment" was pretty intellectual still, and this heartbreak brought me into my emotions, my feelings, with a vengeance. I tell this story in Chapter Six, in the section on forgiveness.

The second event, which marked the last liberation I needed to pass through, was when I filed for bankruptcy. I had had a costly divorce, and had gotten way behind on my credit card bills and tax payments. The IRS was threatening to levy my bank account.

Both my accountant and attorney had been urging me to file for bankruptcy protection for two years, but I resisted. Why? I was afraid of what people would think of me. When I looked this fear squarely in the face, I saw it was keeping me from the one thing I wanted most: inner, spiritual freedom. I realized, in the end, that it was only my ego, my self-image, which cared how people might judge me. Who I really was, my true nature, did not care. I needed to find a way out of my burdensome debt. So, I filed a plan which would allow me to pay what I owed the IRS over a period of years.

Then, in the spring of my forty-ninth year, I woke up one morning feeling mildly depressed. I didn't like what I was feeling. As I lay in bed, I noticed a frustration about still being subject to negative states like depression, even after all these years of spiritual practice. Normally, I would have gotten out of bed and meditated, for I knew how to clear negative energy that way.

But this morning was different. I became very present, looked within, and faced the depression. I was curious. How come such a negative state could still visit me? How come I wasn't completely free yet? Then I remembered Jean's teaching that we are not the psychological/emotional "person." I went deeply into the interior of my being with the question:

"Okay, Jim, you say you are depressed. So, *who* is depressed?"

This wasn't just a mental exercise. This wasn't just some spiritual technique I was toying with. There was a definite urgency to my question. I *really* wanted to know. It was as if my entire life was on the line.

Yet as hard as I looked, I couldn't find the "person" who claimed he was depressed. The more I shone the clear light of awareness inside myself, the more all thought forms, including the thought "I feel depressed," just dissolved. The energy of depression cleared, I felt fine, and went about my day.

But the same thing happened to me the next morning, and the following morning. I awoke and noticed a slightly depressed feeling. Each time I went deeply into myself with the same inquiry—"So, *who* is depressed?"—and after the third morning, something shifted, permanently. Whatever sense of "self" remained in my consciousness dissolved, and I now knew myself as the Whole, as the awareness, or consciousness, behind all thoughts, forms, experiences—indeed, behind all manifest reality.

In the succeeding months, whenever I looked inside myself I couldn't find a solid sense of a "me" anymore. I no longer "believed" my own story, whether it dealt with self-doubt, suffering, still not being free, or a story about my accomplishments, successes, and things in which I took pride. Instead, there was just clarity, openness, and a feeling of emptiness which was simultaneously vibrant, full, and alive.

As the months passed, it dawned on me that I had finally found what I had been seeking for twenty years. What Jean told me, was guiding me towards, was now a bright, integrated reality. I saw once and for all that the psychological/emotional entity called "I" does not exist. My true nature is pure consciousness, expressing through this body, mind, and personality known as "Jim Dreaver."

The difference was, before I awakened to the truth of my being, I was still identified with my ego and thoughts, with my story about who I thought I was, with being "somebody." Now I lived inwardly in luminous clarity, in openness, essentially free of any self-image or self-concept of any kind. I realized that my true nature was, and is, consciousness itself, which never changes.

The Practice Of Self-Inquiry

This practice will help you release identification with the thoughts "I" and "me," and with the ego itself. It will help you make the shift into what some traditions call the observer, or witness consciousness—the awareness that you are *behind* your body, mind, personality, thoughts, stories, sensations, feelings, emotions, etc.

This practice is definitely useful during a time of conflict and suffering, but you can also do it when nothing is going on and you have a quiet moment or two just to look within, and examine this "I," this "me" you take yourself to be.

When conflict, upset, or suffering arises, close your eyes, go within, and ask yourself: "So, who is this 'me' who says he/she is suffering right now?"

Then be very still. Allow whatever feelings or emotions are there to be there. Just be very present and alert, as you search within your psyche, your consciousness, for this "me" who is suffering. Make sure you don't settle for any conceptual answers, which is just more story. You are seeking something tangible: the actual location of the "I" or "me" thought.

After a few minutes of looking into yourself in this way, and as long as you don't get lost in your mind, a truth will dawn on you: you cannot find the "I" or "me" thought anywhere—yet you, as awareness, or consciousness, are still very much here!

What you will discover is that you cannot actually find any thought. This sense of "self" you have been constructing and perhaps struggling with your whole life, can't be found. It doesn't exist, other than as a figment, a fiction, in your mind. Yet consider how much power you have given it to create and control your emotional reality!

So, with this realization, it will become increasingly clear: while you have the thoughts "I" and "me," you are not those thoughts. What you are is the lucid, ever-present awareness *which gives birth to the whole thinking process, and to this body, mind, and personality.*

Seeing this may result in a genuine epiphany, an "Ah ha!" moment. For at least a few moments you will find yourself in a clear, thought-free, present-time awareness. You will no longer experience yourself as an individual "person," but as the universe itself—pure, unbounded consciousness itself, looking through these eyes and expressing through this body/mind/personality that is "you."

Chapter Five

Awakening To Freedom

To know you are not your stories, not even this "I" or "me" you have always taken yourself to be, is true freedom. It's the final perceptual shift resulting in awakening, enlightenment, or self-realization. You no longer seek your identity in the contents of your mind, in the state of your health, or in events or circumstances of any kind, but find it in the moment-by-moment flow of being. No matter what you do, you are always at one with life, you are always in the flow.

The Zen master, D. T. Suzuki, defined enlightenment as: "The lightning-and-thunder discovery that the universe and oneself are not remote and apart, but an intimate, palpitating Whole."

Once you know yourself as the Whole, as one with the dance of the universe, the normal psychological and emotional fears rarely arise. If they do, they occur as brief residues of old ego patterns, rippling on the surface, but not disturbing the deep waters of your inner peace. You just flow with whatever is happening, and deal with it as skillfully and gracefully as possible.

We have seen the wisdom in Idries Shah's statement: "No matter what point of truth or understanding I arrive at, there is always one beyond it." This beautifully expresses the point that the truth—the ultimate answer—does not lie in concepts.

We want to *know* the truth for ourselves, and the practice will bring us to the experience of it. Whenever we feel contracted or stuck we learn to welcome the story and the conflict it produces, because they show us where we are not yet free. We notice the story and realize its impact on our emotional state. Then we become present, and just through watching or witnessing the story it loses some of its energetic hold over us, and we are freer.

As we saw in the last chapter, through deep self-inquiry we confront this "I" at the root of all the stories making up our personal history. We are the witness, the consciousness, the observer looking within, only to discover the ultimate truth: the "I" we were attached to and identified with for so long is not real. It never was.

I like the way Kunihiro Yamate puts it: "Awareness, clarity, a sharp, clear-headed feeling that 'I am awake. This is reality.' That is the way we will feel when we awaken to our full Consciousness."

You know you have awakened to the truth when it becomes stunningly clear to you that not only are you no longer identified with your thoughts, but the very person you took yourself to be—the "me" with all its history—does not exist. In other words, you don't take anything personally because you don't hold onto any idea or image of yourself as a "person."

When you look inside you see only spaciousness and emptiness, an openness you realize is filled with the entire universe. It feels like there's no separate sense of "me" anywhere; you cannot find it because it cannot be found. The entire notion of a "me" is and always was an illusion, a mere concept. "You" cannot be located anywhere, yet you are everywhere. You are this vast, all-encompassing ocean of consciousness.

This realization results in a sense of lightness, freedom, and joy. Your basic state is one of ease, flow, and being alive in the present. All psychological and emotional suffering disappears, never to return—other than those occasional residues, triggered by periods of stress and illness, which can flare up from time to time. Your true purpose for being here becomes clear to you, and living itself takes on a whole new meaning and significance. Truly, every moment is new.

No one else can tell you whether or not you are awake or self-realized. When you look inside, only you can know for sure whether you are inwardly free of conflict, self-doubt, and fear. Only you can know there are no dark, scary places in your psyche anymore, and that thought processes no longer have power over you. There is no longer any separate belief in "I" or "me," but only the light of universal consciousness shining through this body/mind/self appearing as "you."

Ultimately, only you can know whether you are free or not. This is where you have to be very honest with yourself. Another person who is already free can and will recognize and acknowledge your freedom, but only after you yourself have awakened to it.

He or she is able to discern exactly where you are on your path with a few well-placed questions:

"Do you still experience self-doubt?"

"Do you still have any suffering?"

"Are you still identified with an idea or image of 'self'?"

"Does your well-being depend on anything outside yourself?"

The bottom line is, if you are looking to have someone confirm or validate your realization, then you probably are not there yet. However, someone already awake will be able to guide you toward the next step. They cannot take the step for you, but they can direct you towards home.

Along these lines, a woman once expressed her concern to me about awakening being this "carrot in front of a lost and hungry soul." In her view it presented the illusion of some end where all is known, and there is no more to be learned, and therefore, no more growing.

Her words reminded me of the guru myth. It is prevalent in India, common among illiterate villagers, the educated middle-class, and idealistic seekers—the idea of the self-realized teacher, master, or guru knowing everything. Ask him or her a question about economics, computer science, calculus, biotechnology, astrophysics, a foreign language, or what is going to happen in the future, and he or she will know. Moreover, many believe the guru has the power, should he or she choose to use it, to fly through the air, walk through walls, and manifest sacred objects out of empty air.

Obviously, this is just a myth. Awakening to freedom does not mean you know everything or gain magical, reality-defying powers. On the contrary, it means you just know one thing: you truly are "nobody."

Being nobody allows you to live in a relaxed body with a clear, focused mind and a joyful, loving heart. It allows you to be naturally centered and present wherever you are, opening you to accepting all points of view and learning all manner of new information.

Not until awakening happens, until you see through the illusion of "I am this" or "I am that" does the real learning begin. This begins the process of growing into the fullness of your being, the unfolding of your deepest creative potential.

In other words, all concepts and ideas about who you are and what life supposedly means are just barriers to deeper levels of learning and communication. We so often "think" we are growing, but we just go around in circles, getting ever more stuck in whatever story or drama is currently running our lives. Awakening makes you realize how little you actually know, and *this* realization brings you into harmony with the endless beauty, wonder, and mystery of life.

Realizing you are "nobody" and don't have to "try" to be anybody, your body relaxes and your heart opens, making you receptive to the deeper layers of reality unfolding in each moment. Everything you need to know is available to you instantly, even the realization that the timing might not be right for receiving some answers. Sometimes, "later" is the right answer.

When you live in the present, you trust the flow. You are open to the signs and whispers of real intuition and can hear what life and other people are actually communicating to you.

Total trust in the flow is part of your secret. Trust awakens the master within. And while you are unlikely to ever levitate, walk through walls, or manifest objects out of thin air, the small miracles and synchronistic events occurring daily once you come into harmony with existence will definitely bring a quality of magic into your life.

The Power Of Silence

The power of presence is an alertness or heightened awareness which brings you naturally to an inner silence, where the mind is no longer a problem. Jean Klein said: "Be knowingly silent as often as you can." In silence and stillness you hear the hum of creation itself, the Reality behind reality. You sense and experience your true nature, who and what you really are. Listen right now. See if you can hear it. See if you can feel it...

Be very still, eyes open, and tune into the silence within and without... Just listen, and become one with the silence... Notice you are this silence... Your true nature is the silent background to everything... Pure, shimmering stillness, within which all the sounds of creation are heard... Allow yourself to simply enjoy, bask in, the delicious silence of being for a few minutes...

Once in a workshop, a man said: "As I sit here, I definitely do feel—even hear—a kind of vibration, a presence... But I notice there always comes a point when the silence starts to get uncomfortable for me... It's happening now. I start to get restless. My mind says, 'What is this silence?' It's like there's nothing going on and it kind of scares me. Then I want to grab hold of something—some thought, concept, or story."

I told the man this: Observe the tendency of your mind to try and create a thought or story to explain the silence. In acknowledging the story, "What is this silence?" you are brought back into the awareness of the present. This observing or acknowledging is what I have been talking about all along: if you can look at the story you are telling yourself in your mind, then you cannot be the story; you are what is looking at the story. So, just be *it*. This is how simple it is to be who and what you are: consciousness, presence, an energy field which is simultaneously aware of everything, which *is* everything.

Below the surface noise in your mind lies the silence of your true nature. The truest communications come from this place of silent emptiness, which is rich in energy and awareness. When you listen within first and then speak from the silence, your communication with others goes deep. What emanates from silence, ultimately leads back to silence.

The deeper your silence, the stronger your words. Words springing from silence lead to real understanding, and then bring us back to silence itself. They bring us back to the beauty and fullness of *now*, to pure, radiant awareness. Such words bring us to the place where all creation and all love are birthed.

In silence, you feel the vibration of creation itself. You hear the sound of the source, the whisper of eternity. Within the silence, you rediscover your true nature. You experience firsthand that what is manifesting in this individual body, mind, and heart is, indeed, an expression of the one divine power behind the universe. Silence allows you to tap into your deepest creative power, which is no less than the source of all creation, consciousness itself. Silence is healing, nourishing. It is who and what you fundamentally are. In silence you discover the truth of interconnectedness and the priceless jewel of unconditional love.

When you know yourself as consciousness, the source of everything, you carry that inner silence with you as you go out into the noisy marketplace and engage in this wonderful, crazy, ever-fascinating drama called *life*. All awakened individuals share this one quality or characteristic: deep inner silence. It confirms what all the great texts extol: the sage dwells in inner silence.

People who are awake naturally become teachers just by the way they live and interact with others. Regardless of how their worldly activities manifest—talking, laughing, playing, telling stories, engaging in all possible activities—they remain consciously in the depths of the silence. Teaching by example, they walk both worlds simultaneously.

It is not a forced silence, either. Silence unfolds quite naturally when you see all the mental chatter comprising the noise in your mind is entirely self-generated. Seeing your own story, your own incessant thinking getting in the way of your deeper peace and well-being, helps bring everything to a stop. Then the exquisite fragrance of stillness reveals itself. You *are* the stillness.

Most people fill their lives and environment with noise, whether it's music, television, video games, the internet, endless telephone conversations, or being surrounded by other people. For many people, silence can be scary and uncomfortable. Lao Tzu put it this way: "Nothing is more powerful than emptiness, from which people shrink."

Spending time in meditation and contemplation will help you overcome any fear of silence. Instead of running away from your fear, learn to face it. Remember the practice of breathing into it and welcoming it as a teacher and friend.

Of course, the fascinating thing is that true silence is not empty at all. The emptiness out of which all sounds emerge, and back into which they disappear, only appears to be empty. I remember it was David Bohm, the theoretical physicist who was a protégé of Einstein, and a friend of J. Krishnamurti, who said that in one cubic centimeter of empty space, there is the energy equivalent of twenty kilotons of TNT.

So, the silence we start to notice when we get quiet and still is not empty. It is not a lonely and barren place after all. In true silence you discover the energy, the core vibration of creation itself—the hum, the pulse of the Universe. The yogis call it the

Nada, the breath of God. The quieter you get, the louder "It" gets. Buddhists refer to our true nature or emptiness of mind as the plenum-void or the full-nothingness. The silence from which creation manifests has a density and physicality to it. It is teeming with possibility and potential.

To access the gift of awakening, it is vital to take frequent time for inner silence. Until you awaken to its presence within, one of the best places to find it is to go out into nature. Being in nature literally connects you with your inner, essential nature. The experience of being in nature is invariably transforming, healing, and renewing.

There are so many choices: hike up into the hills or mountains, walk in a forest, visit a public park, feel the spaciousness of an open field, or sink in the sand along the seashore. The seashore, of course, is not always so silent, with the waves crashing on the beach, but it is very cleansing. I have often described the experience of going to the wild northern California coast, near where I used to live, as "getting the cobwebs blown out of my system." It is simply very healing to feel the wind blow through you, and to smell the salt air.

Nature, as the Zen master Shunryu Suzuki said, is the true teacher of Zen. Out in nature your consciousness expands beyond the borders of the ego and its story and you begin to merge with the universal consciousness, the larger sense of beingness, which is who and what we all really are. Here, you get a larger, truer perspective on things. I call it the mountaintop perspective, because it leads you toward detachment, so you can see more clearly, more widely.

This is essential for making the shift in perception you are seeking. Instead of being mired in your own story, your own drama, you want to be able to step outside it in order to see that it is not who you really are. Your true nature is consciousness, pure, timeless awareness. Nature helps you discover and connect with it.

Even if you can't go out into nature, you can pause frequently throughout the day—before you open your car door, get up from a chair, make the next phone call, or go into a meeting—to stop, be very present, very still, and remember. You can remember to breathe, feel yourself in your body, be aware of your immediate environment, and open yourself to the stillness, the silence behind all the noises you hear. You can take the time to remember you are not your ego, your story, or your circumstances, but you are the awareness recognizing all of these phenomena.

If you are in a meeting and the other people are open to it, you can invite everyone to share a minute or two of conscious silence. Communing in silence in this way will help everyone present to get on the same energetic wave-length. You will be amazed at the creativity unleashed in the whole group once you start to talk and get into the agenda which has brought you together.

Many years ago I was inspired to write down a short *mantra*. It was my guide in meditation for some time. Listen to the spirit behind it, make it your own, and the secret of those who have found freedom will be yours:

> *The fewer words the better.*
> *Let silence be your teacher.*
> *It is the true power.*

Take A Stand For Truth

Regardless of the spiritual tradition or lineage, if you go deeply into what any true teaching is communicating, you will find it is some variation of this:

"We live in difficult and uncertain times. There is much unrest, fear, and suffering in our world. This fear exists because people feel separate from one another, divided by their social, political, and religious beliefs. More than ever we need to see beyond separateness into the unity, the love which is our true spiritual nature.

"To see beyond separation, or duality, into unity requires a perceptual shift. We realize that while each of us has a personal history, our own self-defining story and beliefs, these are not who we really are. Who and what we really are is the consciousness, the clear, creative awareness, which gives birth to all the beliefs, concepts, and stories. The more we see this—see *from* the perspective of consciousness—the freer we become, and the closer we move to the place where wisdom and love meet."

This truth, the truth of love and unity, is the central message of this book. As you grow in presence, and come to know who you are behind all your beliefs, ideas, and stories about who you are, the truth of awakening will become more real for you. You will come to know yourself as much more than just an isolated "person" in a sea of relatively anonymous people.

You will come to understand you are universal consciousness itself—the Whole—expressing through this unique part, this individual body/mind/self called "you." You will know yourself as the ocean, dancing over the course of your lifetime, in this particular wave form that is your current human incarnation.

With this knowing, you will no longer feel separate from creation or from the rest of humanity. You will feel the interconnectedness of all life, all phenomena, and you will be fearless. You will be free. Then you will live in the world in a way which is true for you. You will be an authentic human being, unafraid to speak the truth, unafraid to express your deepest creative urges. You will follow your bliss, your passion. You will do what you love.

Once I was having a private session with a woman, and she said: "Why is it so difficult to discover and live the truth? I mean, I feel deep down I know what is true for me, but I still have all these fears and considerations going through my mind about why, if I follow my bliss, I am going to fail, or things won't work out. And then, whenever I go to speak my truth, sometimes I can't even get the words out. My voice literally chokes up. I know you are saying these are all just stories, and they are not what I am. I do glimpse my true nature, pure consciousness, in moments. But still, the fears, the choking up, arise."

I responded by saying, "Let's explore it right now. Be present with the choking up. Pay attention to the feelings and sensations. Even welcome them. After all, they are showing you where you are not yet free."

I told her to notice the fears and considerations going through her mind, but don't give them any energy. "Just be present with the whole of your being," I said. "Have your eyes open and all your senses awake. Breathe, and just be with whatever feelings and emotions are there. Be as present and as relaxed as you can be."

"When I do as you say, I must admit I feel more present, more here," she said. "I feel more at ease... But still, the question comes to mind, what about the future?"

"What about the future?"

"Well, what if the fear, or the choking up, happens again?"

"I am sure they will. Even when you fully awaken, residues of the fears that were once so real for you, will surface. They may include the tendency to choke up. When it happens, do exactly what you are doing now. Be present with your experience, and then notice the story, the fear triggering the nervousness, the choking up. You can tell yourself: 'I am *not* my story... I am the pure awareness present right now...' Then be *it*. Be the clear, very present awareness you are. Let the choking up feelings be there, but don't go into your head, don't go into any story about them."

Choking up is a classic fifth chakra symptom. The fifth chakra, the throat chakra, is the center of self-expression. When people are blocked here they can experience a cracking or catching of the voice in the throat and find it difficult to get their words out. They literally struggle to speak their truth. Other physical manifestations, such as a sore or raspy throat, swollen glands, thyroid problems, and chronic neck pain and stiffness can also occur with blockage in the fifth chakra.

When I was a chiropractor, I occasionally saw this occur with women who were married to controlling, dominating men. These women did not feel they could freely express their deepest creative truth. They could not be who they really were because their husbands insisted they conform to some idealized model of "wife," and they were too afraid or too programmed to think or be different. The repressed energy manifested itself psychosomatically in the kinds of problems I just mentioned.

Sometimes, just a woman's plucking up the courage to finally tell her husband to get lost or back off was enough to create a breakthrough and bring about a healing. When we start being honest with ourselves, ridding our lives of the lies and lack of authenticity, it is amazing how much healing happens. As soon as we realize that to *not* express ourselves truthfully, we are actually hurting and making ourselves sick, we are then on the path to freedom. All of a sudden we discover we no longer care what the other person says or does.

I learned a long time ago, in relationships, it is best to tell the truth right at the beginning and risk the small pain of hurt or rejection. If you lie, there will come a point, perhaps weeks, months, or years later, when the deception will be revealed. Once the other person realizes he or she has been deceived all this time, the pain of betrayal goes much deeper, is longer-lasting, and can be devastating.

There is a cleanness, lightness, and openness to living with this depth of truth and honesty. You know what it is like to tell a lie and then have to keep telling it, hoping you remember the story correctly to avoid getting caught. You also know what it feels like to be lied to. Living this way creates suffering for yourself and the other person. It's not liberating at all.

But as you awaken to freedom, you will naturally tell the truth. You couldn't do otherwise. You wouldn't do anything to cause your own suffering, and you wouldn't do anything to cause another to suffer. Practicing being present and truthful frees you from the attachment to your story and brings you closer to genuine freedom.

The Truth Is What Is

Communication, as my friend, Phil Salyer, once said, is the

wonder drug of relationships. And the key to communication is the truth—being willing to hear it and to speak it. It takes courage to speak the truth. The head wants to reason, to be right, and will play all sorts of games in order to be right, but the heart yearns for truth. Without rigorous self-honesty, there can be no awakening, no enlightenment. The truth shall indeed set you free.

There are many reasons why we close down and suppress our aliveness and authenticity. Invariably they have to do with a past history of invalidation, rejection, judgment, ridicule, humiliation, or shame from when we were young. Therapists' offices throughout the country are filled with clients who are struggling to work through these issues.

Psychotherapy is a useful tool for healing the mind and emotions, but without the transpersonal perspective, it doesn't bring about true freedom. You just rearrange the contents in your mind, so you feel a little more at ease, a little more comfortable inside yourself. But you are still a prisoner of your own story. You still believe in the dream world you've created inside your head. The difference is you just now have a bigger prison cell to roam around in.

To be true to yourself means going deeply into your own psyche to see if there is anything you haven't been looking at which needs examining, anything which is blocking your freedom of expression. Then you've got to look and see if there is something you need to say to somebody you haven't said.

The more willing you are to face the truth within yourself, to hear the truth from others, and to speak your truth without fear of the consequences, the more you tap into your passion. You connect with the source of courage within you, the boldness needed to take the risks in life which enable us to achieve great things. Then your destiny, your unique purpose in being here, starts to be fulfilled.

Being willing to hear the truth from others and to speak it confidently is one of the most empowering forms of self-expression available to us. It is one of the most critical skills or practices on the path of awakening. However, the truth is not found by sorting through the beliefs, assumptions, and judgments in your mind. All your mental considerations are what get in the way of truth. They cloud your perception of truth. Knowledge, as Lao Tzu said, is a barrier to truth.

Truth can be defined simply as what *is*. This means if you are hungry, that's what is, and hunger is your current truth. If you are angry, that's what is, and anger, in this moment, is your truth. If you are feeling lonely or afraid, then loneliness and fear are your truth. If you are feeling light and carefree, then this is your truth. If you know, deep inside yourself, that you love to play music, and you must do it on a regular basis, then that is your truth. It is not the only thing that is true about you, but definitely something that is true for you.

The truth, in other words, is whatever is being directly sensed, felt, or experienced. Zen, which is all about living in a true way, speaks of the "suchness" of life. By suchness, Zen masters mean what is, or what is so. The moon is rising. Breathing is happening. The crickets are chirping. Maybe there's a creak in one of your joints when you move. All of these phenomena are the "suchness." They are simply what *is*. If it's late at night, maybe you yawn, and you realize you are tired. That's the truth. It's what is. You're tired.

There is a wonderful and uniquely Zen saying describing the way enlightenment shows up in the world: "Eat when hungry, sleep when tired." Simple! If you understood the deep implications of that saying, there would no longer be conflicts or worries in your life. You would live like a Zen master, fully awake in the present, responding to whatever the situation or the real need in any given moment demands.

And, if there is nothing pressing right now, then you just relax and enjoy the flow of life.

Recognizing Truth

Problems arise not with the situation, but with our interpretation of it. Maybe you get a strange sensation in your chest and you start to panic, thinking you are about to have a heart attack. Or the rent is due in five days and you do not have the money, and you start to do a number on yourself. You begin to create a whole story around what will happen if you can't pay the rent: what your landlord may do, what happens if you get evicted and end up homeless. Maybe you start to shame yourself.

These are examples of what the ego does with what is. It interprets the situation and builds a story around whatever *it* is. Whether it's a pain in the chest, not having the rent money, or uncertainty about a relationship, the ego will create an elaborate drama which often has little basis in fact or reality.

But when you live with what is, when you are in harmony with the suchness of life, there is no need for conflict when a challenging situation presents itself. You just deal with it, you respond. You make whatever changes are needed if you can, or just accept things as they are, but all without building an internal drama around it. Live like this and you are on your way to true freedom.

If, for example, you *don't* have the rent money, tell the truth. No games, just the truth. I remember being late with the rent a few times. I would call the landlord and say, "Look, I'm sorry, but I am going to be late this month." When there is genuinely no fear or embarrassment in your voice, no guilt, no blame, then those you are dealing with will most often relax, too. They open up and are willing to negotiate with you.

Be level headed and responsible. Make payment arrangements or work it out somehow. If the landlord gets angry, it's his or her problem, not yours. You certainly care about meeting your obligations, but you don't worry or lose any sleep if you can't. After all, your financial condition is just that—a condition. On this path, you don't depend on conditions for your well-being. Your happiness comes from a much deeper place. It comes from within you.

If speaking the truth is going to bring actual harm to yourself or to another, if some person or institution would use the information to cause harm, if the truth was cruel or unkind, then you may have to conceal the truth, or some portion of it. Once in a while you may have to downright lie. For instance, if you were a European citizen hiding a Jewish family from the Nazis during the last World War, you would obviously conceal that fact from the authorities.

In some cases, a person may not be ready to face the truth within or about themselves. You may need to tell somebody something, but clearly the outright truth would be crushing to them. Maybe you have to drip-feed it to them. This is where mastery comes in, knowing exactly what to say at any given time, and how to say it. This takes wisdom, discernment, and love.

Now, I often hear this from people: "When I try to listen to what is true inside me, I often hear a number of voices— sometimes a barrage of voices—inside my head. How can I discern my true voice?"

If you take the time to listen carefully, you'll notice that in addition to the many voices that may be echoing around inside your head, there is a voice which resonates from deep down within your gut, your heart, your soul. This is the voice you want to listen to.

I discovered this deeper voice while traveling in Nepal in the early nineteen-eighties. I was staying in a cheap hotel in the tourist section of Kathmandu. I had some hashish, and had smoked some of it, and then had lain on my narrow cot in the hotel room to meditate. As the hashish worked its magic on my mind, I became startlingly aware of two voices inside me.

There was the voice in my head, which was rather shrill, and very mental, and consisted mainly of tape-loops from the past, all my stories, my beliefs, judgments, opinions, and so on. It was what Werner Erhard, the transformational guru who was big in the seventies, called the "yammer-yammer" of the mind.

But there was another voice, one that came from deep inside me. When I got very quiet and still, I could hear this voice. It had a richer and more resonant sound. It felt very authentic, and was very present-time. It was not a voice I could second guess, whereas the first voice, the ego's voice, was very predictable.

The hashish-induced insight into the two voices was an epiphany for me. From then on, I would notice which voice was speaking through me, and I would consciously practice shifting out of my head, down into my body, into a more present-time awareness in which the deeper voice, the voice of truth, could reveal itself.

The more I lived with a heightened sense of awareness and inner silence, I discovered, the more clearly I could hear the voice of truth. Jean Klein always said that true communication comes out of silence, and leads back to silence. If you don't know what to think or say, get very quiet on the inside, and just listen. Be totally present, and listen.

Your true voice will sooner or later reveal itself, in the form of an intuitive insight, a hunch, or maybe a profound thought or phrase that will rise forth into your awareness, seemingly out of nowhere.

Of course, you don't need to smoke hashish to discover you true voice. However, psychoactive drugs, like marijuana, hashish, mescaline, psilocybin, MDMA, and LSD can serve as allies on the spiritual journey. They open the doors of perception and, when used in a sacramental way—i.e. as a conscious ritual— can expand, and sometimes blow, our minds. They can give us an extraordinary taste of the oneness that is our true nature. But they have a dark side, too, and can induce horrific, demonic visions and experiences. So, they are a razor's edge path, and are not to be taken lightly.

For a couple of years in the early nineteen-eighties, I explored psychedelic drugs as a path to awakening, but no longer use them. I do, however, still smoke marijuana occasionally, although I didn't smoke it at all for two years after I experienced the health crisis, when I had the strokes. I didn't want to mess with my delicate brain chemistry.

Once in a while someone questions my use of marijuana, believing that an "awakened" person would not touch it. But for the awakened person there are no rules of conduct, other than do no harm. Marijuana has an established medicinal value. In my case, a couple of arteries in my brain were shutting down because of the strokes. I actually contemplated having surgery, a cranial by-pass, to allow more blood flow. When I started using cannabis again, a brain scan I had done a year afterward showed that those same arteries had opened up a little, so my condition had actually improved.

Many years ago I was sitting on the deck outside my cottage, enjoying the feeling of being stoned. I was thinking about what the word "pot" meant, and had a revelation: it is an acronym which stands for "perception opened totally."

Certainly, that was what it had always done for me. It invariably gave me a rich flow of creative insights which I didn't get in my normal state. The practice in this book, for example, arose out of one such session. It also, of course, enhances kinesthetic sensation, which means it can heighten the experience of activities like movement, dancing, love-making, and listening to or playing music.

But "pot" has another, darker meaning. Your life can go to "pot" if you do it too much. You forget things, make mistakes, and it can destroy the motivation to achieve or accomplish anything. In short, you go *unconscious*. So, *caveat emptor*. Let the buyer beware. As with all things in the material world, balance—just the right amount—is the key to maintaining a healthy, vibrant well-being.

Let's be very clear: any awakening which depends on an agent—be it marijuana or any other drug, or a belief, a story, a circumstance—is, by definition, not a true awakening. True realization shines and stands on its own. The awakened person still has preferences, even habits, but he or she is not bound by any of them.

In fact you could say that awakening or realization is the perfect "high," because there are no negative side effects whatsoever. You feel good all the time...

See if you can hear the voice of truth now...
Welcome whatever you are experiencing right
now, and just be very still, present... Be the

clear, lucid awareness you are... Then look deep
within your body... As that awareness, listen for
whatever voice arising from your heart or gut
wants to be heard... It may say that nothing
is needed right now, or it may voice a need,
something wanting attention... Take note of it,
and then simply be here...

Release Attachment To Outcomes

Some people fear that being awake and living in the now means letting go of goals and dreams, but that is an illusion, a story they have locked onto which keeps them from being present.

The attachment to outcomes, to getting a specific result, sets the stage for anxiety, the fear you won't achieve what you want. As you learn to release the attachment and become genuinely present, new creative energies—as well as feelings of courage and confidence—spring forth, and actually move you closer to your goal.

Worrying about the future is one of the main causes of stress in our lives. It is a habit which just perpetuates fear, the uncomfortable feeling of not being enough as we are. It keeps us stuck believing such-and-such *must* happen if we are going to be happy, and if it doesn't, our lives will be miserable.

A story about J. Krishnamurti speaks with crystal clarity about what it means to be free of this limiting, fear-based pattern of thinking. Every spring for over sixty years he gave talks in a beautiful oak grove in the southern California town of Ojai.

Hearing Krishnamurti speak in person was always an extraordinary experience. His friend, Aldous Huxley, described it thus: "Like listening to a discourse of the Buddha—such authority, such intrinsic power."

It was no less moving when I went to hear him speak in the late 1970's, surrounded by nearly two thousand people in attendance, sitting on the grass or in folding chairs.

Part way through this particular talk, Krishnamurti suddenly paused, leaned forward, and said, almost conspiratorially, "Do you want to know what my secret is?"

Almost as though we were one body we sat up, even more alert than we had been, if possible. I could see people all around me lean forward, their ears straining and their mouths slowly opening in hushed anticipation. Krishnamurti rarely ever talked about himself or his own process, and now he was about to give us his *secret*. Why else did we come to Ojai every spring, but to see if we could find out just what his secret was? We wanted to know how he managed to be so aware and enlightened, while we struggled with conflict and our many problems.

There was a silence. Then he said in a soft, almost shy voice: "You see, I don't mind what happens."

We sat back as we contemplated his words, and considered the whole notion of what it would mean to not mind what happens.

A woman to whom I told this story said: "To me, not minding what happens sounds too passive. It's almost like you're allowing people and life to walk all over you. I mean, I have a five-year old daughter. I would be devastated if something happened to her. I go out of my way to protect her, to take care of her."

I explained to her that without a deeper understanding, it may seem so, yes. The deeper understanding we are talking about, of course, is inner freedom, total awakening. In the poem, *Little Gidding*, T. S. Eliot described the awakened state as a "condition of complete simplicity, costing not less than everything."

Therefore, you have to let go of everything in your mind to be truly free. To use Krishnamurti's phrase, you have to not "mind" what happens, and including your inner attachment to your daughter's well-being. But you are still human. You love your daughter and will naturally care for her and protect her. You just won't be obsessing about it or always thinking about it, which gives rise to the specter or paranoia about being devastated at the thought of possibly losing her.

Being awake does not mean you lose the normal human desires and preferences. You still feel and honor your creative urges. You still set out to do whatever you really want to do with your energy. If you don't like the circumstances you find yourself in, by all means take action to change them if they can be changed. The difference is they are now just circumstances, not problems.

Outwardly, for example, you might need to fiercely cling to a goal or objective in order to see it through to a successful conclusion. Yet inwardly, if you are truly free, there is no emotional attachment to what happens. You know yourself *as* the field of awareness, of presence. This knowing, and the enduring peace it brings, is not dependent on whether you achieve your goals or not.

In other words, you are passionately committed to your goals and intentions, but you are ultimately unattached to the outcome. This freedom from attachment liberates you from fear, from worrying about whether you are going to succeed or not. When you take the worry out of your work you are actually more likely to succeed.

The process is exactly the same as the earlier example of how a Zen master climbs a mountain. Whether it's to make more money, learn a new skill, explore a new city, or attain enlightenment, first, set your goal, your intention, and then put it at the back of your mind and focus on the journey. Pay attention to the step you are taking right *now*. This is the best way to ensure your next step will be successful.

It is a timeless spiritual truth: release attachment to outcomes, and deep inside yourself, you will feel good no matter what. You feel good because you are connected to the energy of the universe, the beauty and power of creation itself. You will be one with the silence behind it all, and therein lies the true power...

*Be one with the silence now... Be very alert
and present, immersed in the flow of creation...*

Notice how you, as consciousness, are still very much here… Yet, right now, in this very moment, there is no need to think or to worry about the future… Soon, you can think about what you need or want to do, but right now, it is enough just to be the beautiful, present-time awareness you are…

The Proof Your True Nature Is Consciousness

In a workshop, a man said: "I understand that while I have a personal 'story,' a psychological and emotional history, it is not who I really am. But what about cultural and ethnic identities? I am a Jew, and the whole of Jewish history makes me who I am. It is in my blood, my genes. I have a Muslim friend I've known since childhood who says the same thing about her background. Yet you say consciousness, and not my Jewishness, is my true nature. Can you prove this to me?"

I replied: "Without doubt your Jewishness is part of your personal story and your family history, your genetic lineage, so to speak. The body is what it is, the genes are what they are, and even the cultural conditioning is imprinted to a certain degree. But you don't have to be at the effect of any of this. After all, you are *conscious* of being Jewish, right?"

"Yes."

"That proves my point," I said. "Consciousness, the awareness of body, mind, senses, and identity, comes *first*. Consciousness is the ground of being giving rise to all thoughts, sensations, beliefs, and experiences. No matter what is happening in your experience, no matter what you identify with, you are *aware* of it. Awareness, or consciousness, is primary. The practice we have been doing all along helps us come to this realization."

The difference between awakened and unawakened people is the former live from the ultimate Reality, the nondual reality. They dwell in awareness, in pure, silent consciousness itself, all the while acknowledging the relative reality of thoughts, beliefs, feelings, and experiences, including racial, ethnic, and religious differences, as well as genetic lineage.

Because they live from and embrace the ultimate perspective, the context of the whole, they are able to honor and work with the content, the day-to-day events and circumstances, without getting lost in it. By seeing the big picture, they see the intrinsic inter-relationship of all the parts.

On the other hand, unawakened people are caught up in the relative reality, in the content, in one or more of the parts. Not having opened to and connected with the ultimate Reality, the consciousness which is the source of all thought, sensation, and feeling, they cling to what can be seen, felt, experienced.

This includes all the beliefs people hold onto regarding the value of a particular ethnic, national, religious, cultural, or social identity. When you factor in the personal history, all the subjective memories from the past, both painful and pleasant, you have this world between the ears I call "me, myself, and my story."

As long as people cling to their story or version of reality, be it Jewish, Muslim, Christian, Buddhist, Hindu, black, white, or gender oriented, there is going to be conflict and suffering within and between individuals and groups. Conflict and suffering are then projected outwardly in various forms of religious, political, ethnic, and social strife. There is a resistance to the natural flow, the ups and downs of life. People are unable to see the truth: a *story* about something is not the truth of it.

It is happening right now all around the world in various hot spots of conflict and war. Human beings have been clashing and fighting with each other since they first learned how to wield a stick and throw a spear. Back then, they didn't even have religious stories to do battle over, but they had survival stories, they had stories of their clan or tribe.

A question I sometimes get asked when talking about the violence in the world is: "What's your solution, then? Surely you don't expect people to give up their Jewish, or Muslim, or Christian, or Hindu identities?"

I responded by saying it would be a huge step to at least give up the *attachment* to those identities. It would change the world if a large number of us began being more interested in what was actually, scientifically proven to be true—i.e. the primacy and universality of consciousness—rather than the ethnic, cultural, nationalistic, or religious stories we've been programmed with down through the ages. Then we would experience a lot less war, and a lot more peace.

You can still honor any and all of your religious traditions, for tradition is a beautiful thing. However, it is important to see the inherent limitations in being attached to those traditions. If we try to overlay traditional values and ideals on whatever the current reality is, such an overlay prevents us from opening to something deeper, fresher, and newer in the present. We remain caught in duality and conflict.

The Role of Religion In A Conscious World

As people throughout the world awaken to the truth within them, religion itself, regardless of its form or expression, will undergo a transformation.

Because of the awakening, or flowering of consciousness, religion will become a much more genuine expression for those who now pay homage to it. Instead of religion telling us how to live, we will shape *it* to serve us, to serve all of humanity, fully honoring the original beauty, truth, and goodness which initially gave birth to the religion.

After all, we created religion in the first place. Since we made up the story, we can revise it in any way we choose.

Religion, as I see it, has two vital functions. The first is the way in which it gets us started on the spiritual path, and offers us a helping hand, moral support, and guidance along the way. This is where our priests, pastors, rabbis, and mullahs can become important guides for us. The more awake they are, and the less caught up in the story, in dogma and rules, the more they can serve us by helping us see the light.

I am referring, of course, to the true light, the light of

our innermost being, not just the reflected light glancing off the cross, sparkling on the chalice, or streaming through the stained glass window. These emanations of light off or through sacred objects are always beautiful to behold, but it is ever important to remember where the light comes from, otherwise we get seduced by objects and images outside ourselves. The light comes from the Source, of course. It comes from within us. We *are* the light.

The second great function of religion is community. Community brings people together, not just to worship the Source, the power behind creation, but to deal with conflict and crisis. When disaster, natural or man-made, strikes a community, the church, temple, or mosque becomes a rallying point, a center for collecting and focusing the energy, money, and talents of all those who have come to lend a hand. It becomes a resource for handling the logistics and supplies needed to address the particular crisis. It becomes a haven for sharing the burden of suffering, for giving and receiving physical, emotional, and spiritual sustenance and support.

During times of upheaval or disaster, or simply when there is a community need, governments are often ineffective or even powerless to help. It is ordinary people, concerned people, people of faith and compassion gathering at their local place of worship, who make the real difference.

So, awakening doesn't mean religion will go away. It just means religion will change, will undergo a transformation. Religion itself will become enlightened. Given the dark side of its history, all the death, terror, and suffering it has inflicted upon humanity in the name of "God"—and still does, in many parts of the world—such a change will be a good thing.

Many people wonder about prayer, and how that changes as we awaken more to our true nature. Instead of praying to some idea of God or a higher Power, you will be supremely alert in the present, fully attentive in this moment now, and you will *feel* as a palpable reality the immense silence behind creation. You will feel the power of it vibrating in every cell of your being, and you will know, beyond a shadow of a doubt, the "Power" you once prayed to actually exists. It is the very substratum of existence, the very energy and consciousness of which you are made.

Then your prayers will take on a different tone. Rather than beseeching or asking, you will be expressing the gratitude you feel for the grace continually being bestowed upon you, and upon all who have the eyes, the ears, and the sensitivity to notice it.

Instead of living in fear of not being "saved," not being "good enough" to make it to Heaven when you die, or not belonging to the "right" religion, you will realize everything is perfectly okay. You will realize everything has *always* been perfectly okay. Heaven is here now, despite the seeming hell misguided human beings create.

It is just as Jesus said: "The kingdom of God is within you." Or as the Sufi masters put it: "God and heaven live within your own heart." Or as the yogis and sages have always known: "Bliss, peace, and happiness are your true nature."

Grace Rains Down

With awakening there comes a profound sense of peace, trust, and happiness—a happiness not dependent on conditions or circumstances, but shining on its own, the very expression of the beautiful, conscious being you really are.

Personal conflict, fear, and discontent leave you, because you no longer take yourself to be a "person." Rather, you have no concept or image of yourself making you need to proclaim, whether to yourself or others: "I am this," or "I am that."

You don't go through the day thinking about yourself in the old way anymore. You're just being what you are: pure, divine awareness, expressing through this body, these eyes, and this mind which others perceive of as "you." If you think about anything at all it is just to remember to be present, should you get momentarily distracted, caught back up in a residue of your former "self."

You still have your own unique personality and temperament, but now you are much more open, spontaneous, and authentic. Your personality is no longer rigid, reactive, and predictable as it was when you were caught up in a story about who you thought you were.

With awakening, your work and unique destiny become clear. You live each day, each hour, in gratitude for the gifts, big and small, which life continually showers upon you. Jean Klein always said that as we get freer, gratitude becomes our predominant emotion. Without a doubt, this has been my experience.

The nineteenth-century Bengali saint, Ramakrishna, said it slightly differently: "Grace rains down ceaselessly."

This grace is always available. Consciousness is who and what you are. Grace is your true nature. God is not out there in some place or state as you were taught when you were young, but is the very substance of your being. God *is* consciousness. Consciousness is God.

Understanding this is what frees you from the fear of death. As you see the truth of everything more clearly and release the attachment to the rigid identification with "I" and "me" you come to the realization, nobody is born and nobody dies. As a historical person you exist only as an idea or concept inside your head. Your body is born, yes, but you are not your body. You are the consciousness giving birth to the body, the consciousness which brings it into being, into awareness.

When your body dies, it dissolves into dust, but the consciousness you *are* was not born, and does not die. Consciousness has always been here, endlessly incarnating, endlessly becoming aware of itself, endlessly manifesting in new forms, in new bodies. "You" are an individualized expression of divine consciousness, just as a wave is an expression of the ocean. But, like the wave, your true, timeless nature is the ocean, it *is* consciousness.

When you know yourself as consciousness, you realize that you—as consciousness—have been here since the beginning of time. Your body, mind, and personality will die, but consciousness itself does not die. How can there be an extinction of consciousness? To know you are extinct, you would have to be aware of it—and if you are aware, you're not extinct! And if you're not aware of being extinct, or aware of anything else, then you're not aware of anything period, so clearly there is nothing to be afraid of or to worry about.

It is just like deep sleep. When you wake up from deep, dreamless sleep, you always feel wonderfully refreshed, so if death were a kind of deep sleep, and then you woke up somewhere else, why would it be any different? Whether you wake up back in this realm, in a new body, or in some other realm, in an angelic form, you're always going to feel refreshed. And if you never do wake up, then you don't know anything about it, so again, what is there to fear?

This is the freedom, the liberation, the cosmic sigh of relief that awakening brings. Instead of fearing death, we look upon it as the last great adventure of this particular incarnation. We may even welcome it, when the time comes, with an attitude of: "Well, *this* is going to be interesting…!"

This realization about consciousness not being separate from birth, life, or death brings with it an awesome responsibility. It means we can no longer look to a God out there for help or salvation, nor can we blame a God out there for what has gone wrong in our lives. God is us. Human beings created the whole concept of "God," and made Him in our image. It's just a word, a story we dreamed up to describe the indescribable power and intelligence of the consciousness behind everything.

Once we see and experience the truth of consciousness, our work here becomes clear. It is to guide others, those who are receptive, on the journey of awakening. Maybe we do it directly by sharing the practice and teaching with them. Maybe we do it indirectly, by example, the way in which we embody consciousness and presence in our everyday lives.

Jean Klein put it this way: "In my teaching one points directly to consciousness, the natural state, becomes established in it and then moves down, so to speak, to the transforming of the relative nature."

This transforming of the relative nature, of bringing the consciousness we are into every realm of daily life, is work which will go on till the day we die. After all, who can say they have mastered the art of living? I can't. In terms of living in the world, the marketplace, the learning goes on.

In many people who wake up, a fragment of the old "self" often reasserts itself and gets attached to the idea it is now enlightened—the ultimate ego trip, you might say. This happened to me, and it has happened to other teachers I know.

In Zen they call it "the stink of enlightenment." It's a phenomenon especially prevalent among men, who by nature are competitive and think they need to be one-up on everyone else, even in the spiritual field.

But eventually you see through the "I am enlightened" story too. You let go of the attachment to ideas of enlightenment, to yourself as the messenger, as the one who knows and who has arrived. Now you can just focus on the message. Not so much talking about it, but just *being* it. Being the knowing is what really matters.

A Practice For Being Awake

Take a minute or two right now to just be silent, alert, and aware of whatever is. Be present with whatever you are experiencing. Notice the stories, thoughts, and images passing through your mind, and realize you are not *any of them. What you are is the consciousness, the awareness, which permeates your body, mind, and personality, and which sees everything.*

If you like, you can affirm to yourself: "I am not my story. My true nature is pure consciousness manifesting in this body, mind, and personality that is me..." Then let the thought go, take a deep, conscious breath, and relax into being the pure, silent awareness you are.

When you are present like this, seeing without any story whatsoever, you are free. Everything in your universe, including all that you choose to create, flows out of this moment now...

Chapter Six

The Power Of Love

With the awakening to our true nature as consciousness, each day becomes rich in love, meaning, and purpose. In this chapter I want to speak about love.

Love, after all, is the most important and vital emotion we human beings can feel. The East Indian sage, Ramakrishna, said: "The mind will take you into the courtyard of the Beloved, but only the heart will get you into the bedroom."

Love is what humanity needs to show more of if there is ever to be any kind of a global healing. Since long before the time of Jesus, whose teaching was all about love, prophets and sages have been telling us we need to love each other more. Yet people everywhere seem to struggle with loving one another as much as they struggle internally with everything else.

Modern psychology is on the mark when it says we must learn to love ourselves first and then we can love others. But so long as we remain in the realm of the psychological and emotional, it is not so easy. There is the "self" we think we are, and the "self" we are trying to improve, to love. It can be very confusing—as it usually is, when we are still identified with the personal, when we cannot see beyond our own ego concerns.

Through doing the three-step practice I have been presenting here, through embodying the teaching that you are not your story, you are led to the understanding that there is just one energy, one universal consciousness manifesting in an endless diversity of forms. You are *that* energy, and its very nature, as it is expressed through the human heart, is love.

Reality is an indivisible Whole. Every living creature is a wave flowing out of and receding back into the one ocean of creation. Connecting with the oneness or wholeness of life paves the way for opening the heart. When you realize all fears are self-created, there is a deep relaxation or letting go at the somatic level. Then your heart will naturally feel the flowering of goodness, kindness, and love.

This is the very essence of love—to open our hearts and tap into our true compassion. It is to feel our energetic oneness, our interconnectedness, with every other human being and every living thing. However, in most of us, this flowering in the heart needs to be nurtured and brought forth.

The more we feel it the more we extend our love outwards, and the more our actions are governed by such heart qualities as empathy, kindness, affection, tenderness, compassion, forgiveness, generosity, gratitude, and courage.

This is where enlightenment comes down from the mountaintop and enters the marketplace. What I call the "mountaintop view" describes time spent in meditation, contemplation, and self-inquiry to discover our true nature— the wisdom, love, and freedom inside us.

But this awakening to truth, to the divine love within oneself, is only the first step. Our ability to bring this love down from the mountaintop into the marketplace is the test of how deep and real our awakening is. It reveals our ability to be there with and for others; it shows the degree to which our heart is truly open.

Inner freedom is absolutely attainable. Once you are free, you are always free. Other than those minor residues or echoes from the past occasionally cropping up, there is no getting stuck again. Residues are most likely to occur when the body is going through pain or illness of some kind, or survival is being threatened in some way.

But the mastery of love is something else altogether. In a way, we are all beginners at love. Mastery of your mind brings you to the experience of clarity and detachment, of freedom and openness, of spaciousness and presence. But opening and awakening the heart brings you into intimacy with life and with people.

As your heart opens and fear dissolves, your chest literally expands and is filled with warmth and love. This feeling of expansion is the sign that consciousness is entering your heart. When you trust and live from your heart your true passion is liberated. The heart is the true healer.

Practical Love

Nisargadatta Maharaj said: "Wisdom is knowing I am nothing, love is knowing I am everything, and between the two, my life moves." This is a beautiful expression of truth.

As you awaken you will indeed discover you are "nothing" and "everything." In that discovery, you will feel the power of the universe moving through you, and realize you are connected to everyone and everything. True freedom arises in the knowing, which is articulated as wisdom, and the feeling, which is expressed as love.

Life then becomes very rich because now you are connected to the love within you, to the power of the universe itself. You still welcome love from other people—after all, you want to see the whole world awaken to this love within—but you no longer *need* it. The light and love shining in you are strong enough now. In fact, they overflow, such that you cannot help but share your radiant, loving presence with those who are open and receptive to it.

When I talk about love in this way, I often get this question: "What you are saying sounds true, but I still find it very hard to love certain people. I think many others would find it hard to love, too. I mean what about terrorists whose sole purpose is to kill and destroy? Are we supposed to love them? Or, closer to home, how can you expect a mother to love her child's murderer?"

We have to look at love from a very practical perspective. Love is not necessarily about liking every human being on earth, or even your neighbor, especially if he or she is mean-spirited, malicious, or ill-willed. It is not about condoning harmful or destructive behavior.

And even though people may be partially or almost totally disconnected from it, love *is* fundamentally about respecting the inherent humanity of all people, and looking for the spark of truth, goodness, and light residing somewhere deep within everyone's heart and soul.

The ongoing work of awakening is to bring love from inside your heart out into the world where it can make a difference. Learning to do this is a lifelong process. It requires you to be very conscious and aware throughout the day. When you notice you are not being aware, when you are caught up in distraction, in judgment, in some story, take that as your cue to come back to awareness. Take it as your reminder to come back to being here now.

You have to be vigilant. Sometimes you might have to remind yourself to listen more carefully, to be more compassionate, to reach out and put your arm around someone. You may have seen through the illusion of the "person," of your own story, but opening the heart is an endless process. It is a journey of growing *into* love, of learning to express your true, compassionate nature ever more fully. It's about being very aware, present, open, and grounded in your body in each moment.

As freedom becomes more real for you, being centered and grounded happens naturally and effortlessly. From this place you can reach out and share who you are with others. You can open your heart to them. If there's an invitation to speak or someone asks you a question, you can introduce the awakening conversation. Above all, you will be able to share your silence, your stillness, and your peace.

As often as possible and as much as you can, let yourself be guided by awareness, presence, and love, and one day true freedom will be yours. Then you will know how to act and what to do—even in the face of a terrorist act, even if, God forbid, your own child were murdered.

The Religion Of The Heart

A man once said to me: "I want to open my heart more. I often feel a kind of tightness in my chest which I am sure is fear. The doctors told me there is nothing wrong with me physically, so I know it is not organic. You have given us a good practice for facing fear, the story around it. I have been doing that and the fear is definitely lessening. Is there anything more you can tell me?"

Tightness in the chest is the somatic or physical manifestation of a heart which, at times, is still closed. It is a sign of an unresolved fear. The first step is learning to really welcome, or at least accept the fear from the perspective that it is showing you where you are still not free. It also helps to live inwardly with the question, "What am I afraid of?" and then notice what images, intuitions, and flashes of insight come into your awareness during the day.

Heart chakra issues become obvious in relationships so pay particular attention to what happens whenever you are with people. Relationships test your ability to give or receive love.

You will probably find the fear has to do with rejection, issues of abandonment or entrapment, or being hurt or judged in some way. Like all such fears, it can be traced back to a pattern of emotional wounding in childhood. The more you learn to face the fear, to meet it head on, the more insight you will get into how and why it has been running the story of your life all these years.

Then, as you realize you are not your story around fear, the freer you will become. No matter how true the story once was, you will know with increasing certainty that you are the awareness, the field of presence which watches or looks at the story *now*. You'll find yourself relaxing into your true nature.

As you learn to be the beautiful, conscious person you are, the fear will drop away. While it definitely feels like a real emotion, it is based upon an illusory story and cannot exist in the light of truth, of your presence.

> *Take a few minutes to meditate on this right now... Look within... Notice that inside your head you may have old memories surface, stories around childhood wounds and fears... And then corresponding emotions and feelings in your body... Let the story and the feeling or emotion be there, in the vastness of the awareness, the consciousness you are... These stories and feelings come and go, but who and what you really are—this spacious, luminous, and loving awareness—is timeless and ever-present... It is your true nature... So be that... Be who and what you really are...*

Fear, the barrier to love, has its roots in beliefs and the stories around those beliefs. People believe in some things so fervently they are willing to die, or kill, for what they believe. In Jed McKenna's book *Spiritual Enlightenment: The Damnedest Thing*, which is an excellent depiction of the nondual approach, he says:

"It's amazing how desperately we cling to our beliefs. As history shows, the fastest way to reduce otherwise decent, caring people to a state of savagery is by tampering with their belief system. The word for someone who does so is heretic, and the punishments reserved for him are more heinous than for any other type of criminal."

He describes people who are identified with their stories and beliefs, people who are not at all open to anything new or different. Awakening, on the other hand, is all about getting beyond the stories and beliefs. It is about seeing those stories and beliefs to which we cling are not even real. They are just concepts, assumptions about truth. Yet notice how, when it comes to religion especially, people are willing to fight, kill, and die for their beliefs.

This was the Christianity of the Crusades and the Inquisition. With the Inquisition a hint of heresy meant you could be tortured in a horrible way. Just imagine Jesus' reaction had he seen what the church did with his teaching of love! However, Christianity had two thousand years in which to mature. Islam, by comparison, is a younger religion, and its fundamentalist elements display their own alarming degree of savagery when it comes to dealing with what the mullahs judge as heresy.

It is tragic and absurd when you think about it, stoning someone to death because they don't agree with your story about God and creation, or because they have different sexual tendencies, or do something forbidden by some "authority's" interpretation of the rules of your religion or society.

Technologically, we live in an age of enlightenment, but there's still incredible darkness, prejudice, and bigotry in the world—all because people are caught up in believing some myth, some story about God and the meaning of life.

The most dangerous kind of religious fundamentalism thrives in places where there is extreme poverty, where there is both economic and social injustice. The fundamentalist religious cause becomes a rallying cry, and brings meaning to otherwise hopeless, despairing lives. As the economic and social inequalities are righted, people become more interested in balance and moderation as a way of preserving and perpetuating the good they are now beginning to enjoy.

But adjusting outer conditions and circumstances, while important, is just one level of freedom. At the deepest level, it comes down to making the adjustment individually—finding personal freedom.

Freedom starts right here, with each of us. Come back to your own situation, your own suffering, and inquire as to what is needed for *you* to free yourself. When you find freedom, you will no longer live in fear. The more of us who realize genuine inner freedom, the more this truth will spread outwards in our world. Then, depending on your gifts and talents, you will make your contribution toward a more conscious world.

If you are a scientist, you will find a way through science. If you are a lawyer, you will find it through seeking justice for worthy causes. If you are a corporate CEO, you will build a corporation which values more than just the bottom line, which pays attention to the well-being of its employees, its customers, and the environment. If you are a politician, you will pursue policies that help transform our communities and our nation.

If you are a priest, a rabbi, a pastor, or a mullah, you will take what is genuinely good and true in your religion, and you will share it with your congregants. But you will not fill their heads with dogmas and threats of hell and damnation, which only makes their hearts heavy and fearful.

When asked about his religion, a teacher of mine from India named Dada said: "My religion is the religion of the heart."

I have always remembered those words. When you practice presence and awareness and awaken to your true nature as consciousness, your heart opens. Then kindness, love, and generosity become the natural cornerstones of your behavior.

If everyone observed the religion of the heart, the world would be a beautiful and safe place for all of us. There would be room to express our competitive, striving nature in a healthy way because it would be balanced by cooperation and sharing. If we lived like this we wouldn't be in the fragmented place in which we find ourselves.

How, then, to practice the religion of the heart? Magrabi Sahib, a spiritual master also from India, gave us this exquisite prescription:

"When I looked in I found within me that which has been sought for ages by all mankind. We have been searching for it for many ages here and there, from one corner of the earth to the other, but we have found it only in our heart. Therefore do not search for your lost Beloved outside yourself. You will find Him (or Her) only in the recess of your heart."

Discover The Healing Power Of Forgiveness

Forgiveness, simply defined, is the letting go of blame or resentment toward anybody who has hurt, offended, or slighted you in the past.

So long as you are still living from your ego, story, or image about who you are, you will always be subject to being hurt. Sooner or later, someone will do or say something to offend you. Then you will live with the feeling of being hurt, and of being angry because you were hurt, for some time. Some people nurse their hurt feelings and anger for weeks or months, while others do it for years or decades.

However, if you are on a path of personal or spiritual growth you will, at some point, realize the hurt and anger you are holding onto are actually causing more harm to you than they are the other person. The other person is merrily going on with his or her life (which just pisses you off even further!) and here you are, suffering miserably because of what he or she said or did months or years ago.

But you can't deny it any longer. You've heard about forgiveness, you've read about it, and as much as you may hate doing it, you finally realize, for your own sanity and well-being, you're going to have to get over it. You're going to have to let go. So, how do you do that? There are exercises, practices, and visualizations for learning to forgive. Let me share with you one of the most powerful practices I used to let go of my own hurt feelings and anger.

A few years before I awakened to my true nature, I met and fell in love with a much younger woman who fulfilled all my ideas about what a perfect mate would be like. That was undoubtedly my first mistake, all the projections I made! I fabricated a whole story in my mind about who she was and what she represented to me. To a large degree she became my identity. Thus I suffered terribly when I felt her disappearing from my life!

Also, the whole idea of "falling" in love suggests a kind of unconsciousness. Better, I think, to consciously grow *into* love with someone. Anyway, I had yet to learn those lessons.

After two years my girlfriend fell in love with someone closer to her own age and this precipitated the end of our relationship. Since she failed to tell me about this other man, there were lies, deceptions, and betrayals. I was heart-broken and ended the relationship just to keep my sanity intact. I had fallen head-over-heels for this young woman. I had become so completely identified with the story I'd fabricated around her that I experienced a tremendous emotional pain when it all fell apart.

Yet as painful as the experience was, I knew it was necessary. My awakening, such as it was at the time, was pretty intellectual and quite detached. Going through the emotional pain brought me into my heart, into my feelings, into reality with a vengeance. Even during the worst of it, which lasted a couple of months, I knew it was for my highest good.

The phrase going through my mind at the time was: "God is giving me a much-needed lesson in pain and feeling."

Surprising me the most was the feeling of anger which began to roil away inside me. While getting over the shock of her betrayal, I experienced an anger I never felt before, the kind which screamed inwardly, "How *dare* she do this to me!" I even found myself contemplating murderous thoughts. I am sure just about every spurned lover has felt something akin to this. It is the stuff of great drama.

In fact, it is the kind of drama that is best left for television, the stage, the pages of a novel, or the cinema screen. However, until we wake up to the beautiful, conscious people we really are, we seem destined to act out these dramas in real life.

I dealt with my anger and pain by going to the Sonoma Mountain Zen Center for a week. I rented a small cabin, I ate my meals with the others there, and meditated a few times in the *zendo*, the meditation hall, but mostly I just sat by myself in the cabin and took long, meditative walks around the beautiful property.

I sat with my feelings and welcomed everything which came up. Sitting on my *zafu*, my meditation cushion, in the tiny, little cabin in the woods, I sometimes felt very vulnerable, sobbing over the loss of this woman I loved. At other times I felt almost self-righteous. I'd view her with scorn and envision ways I could take out my anger on her. I gave myself free reign to do all this. It was what I needed to do for my healing.

Then there were times when the feelings of loss and anger would pass, leaving me sitting in clear, almost blissful freedom as I came home to myself. I was able to let go of all thoughts and images of her and simply rest in stillness, in the beauty and fullness of *being*.

These clearer moments helped me to realize she had her own issues and was just following the call of her soul. She didn't hate me. She just needed to move on, and I needed to let her go. This brings me to the specific forgiveness process I wanted to share with you:

I visualized her standing before me as I surrounded her with light and wished her well. Inwardly, I thanked her for the gifts she brought into my life, and wished her all the best for her journey.

One of the keys to forgiveness is realizing the person who hurt you is only acting out of their own belief system, their own story of need and suffering. In the case of my former girlfriend, she was still exploring and trying to find herself. If I was the lover of inner truth and freedom I said I was, who was I to try and stop her? Heck, my whole life was about supporting people in waking up. This realization helped me get over my own pain fairly quickly.

Coming to the realization you are suffering and you want to be free from suffering more than anything else is the heart and soul of forgiveness. Your suffering is the result of the anger, hurt, and blame—the story—you are holding onto. You are smart enough to see if you act out your anger, if you dump it on the person who hurt you, it is going to perpetuate the cycle of suffering—for yourself, and the other person. You might feel a certain pleasure in acting out your anger, but so long as you remain attached to your self-righteous story, you will continue to attract people who offend or hurt you.

In the end, you come face-to-face with the cold, hard truth of the matter: you have to let your blame and self-righteousness go. You might practice kissing or waving goodbye to it, or visualize wrapping the anger and hurt in a silk cloth and tossing it into an imaginary fire. Do whatever works for you.

Ultimately though, it always comes back to the direct path. You breathe deeply, shrug your shoulders, and metaphorically shake off whatever you're holding onto which is not you. You become supremely present, relaxed in your body, your heart open. You are right here in this moment—aware, alert, awake.

Through the power of clear, present-time awareness, you reconnect with the true beauty and vastness of life. You feel the energy of the universe moving through you again. You realize you are one with the universe. You *are* the universe.

In this oneness, all feelings of separation, hurt, and anger eventually dissolve and are replaced by clarity, light, presence, and a great feeling of peace...

Be the oneness right now... Go within and visualize your body as vast, empty space, space which is at the same time infinitely full... Connect with your heart, the love breathing within you, the love you are... Now think of someone who has hurt or betrayed you in the past... See them, the image of them, enveloped by the love you are... Whatever their intention was, they were clearly misguided... They were operating out of their own inner demons... Thus, it is easy for you now to forgive them... Send them love, radiate love to them as you breathe out slowly, and then let the image of them go... Now just be here, as the awareness, the presence you are...

As you do this practice of being the loving awareness you

are, a wonderful, relaxed feeling of ease, spaciousness, and well-being may unfold within you. Remember: you can't hold onto this feeling, or keep it, because it is what you most essentially *are*. It is your natural state. So don't try.

If you feel yourself contracting—getting caught in conflict, stress, or upset—it is your cue to come back to presence. It is in presence, in the awareness of being here right now, that you re-discover your true universal nature. But to fully and completely awaken, you must inquire into who you are. You must investigate the "I." You must look deep within to find its source or origin.

No matter how deeply you look, you'll discover you cannot find it. Your "I," your ego, has no reality in and of itself. Only consciousness is ultimately real. This is the great liberation those who have awakened come to. This is the key to unlocking the secret of inner freedom.

Love Unconditionally

Toward the end of my time at the Zen Center I felt much better, much clearer, more truly in a place of forgiveness. I processed all my feelings, and by and large, they fell away. The falling away or letting go is the essence of forgiveness. In the space opened up, a whole new creative energy began to pour through me.

Somewhere around the same time, I read a book, *The Chasm of Fire*, by a Sufi teacher named Irina Tweedie. The book is about her studies with a Sufi master in a small village in India—all her trials and difficulties, her amazing energy experiences, and her insights and breakthroughs.

On the first page of the book she says: "Only a heart which has burned itself empty is capable of love."

This is a beautiful statement of truth. We have to empty ourselves of everything—our ego, personal history, our story of suffering and blame—and then we can, at last, open to the flowering of love. Then love can move through us.

In most traditional spiritual paths, and in the psychological approach, this emptying happens progressively as you practice releasing the past and forgiving those who have hurt you. But in the direct path approach, the letting go happens naturally and effortlessly as you see what you were holding onto isn't even real.

Through doing the three-step practice, and through contemplating the teaching, you realize that if you can observe the stories, beliefs, and images causing you to suffer, you cannot *be* them. You are the vast, timeless awareness which observes and experiences.

Be who you are, then. Dwell in the freedom, clarity of mind, and openness of heart which is your true nature. Then the love flowing through you will always be unconditional for there is no "you" in it, no ego self laying down rules, expectations, conditions, or agendas.

You just love because you love, plain and simple. What others do with your love is up to them. Those whose hearts are sufficiently open and whose level of trust is deep enough, will accept your love, appreciate it, and reciprocate. Those whose hearts are closed will not be able to receive the gift you have to give them. But it's okay. Remember, there are no conditions on your love. Maybe they will be ready next time.

The freer you are and the more your heart opens, the more naturally you feel compelled to reach out and connect with your fellow human beings. Because we are all part of an indivisible Whole, you feel their suffering, but you don't take it personally.

I remember the British novelist and philosopher, Aldous Huxley, saying something beautiful about the interconnectedness of all people. He was comparing Christ's famous injunction to "Love your neighbor as yourself" with the great phrase from the Hindu Upanishads, "You are That."

Jesus was probably the greatest master of the way of the heart our world has ever seen. And his teaching was essentially nondual, as evidenced by his statement: "I and the Father are one," the word "Father" being a metaphor for consciousness.

However, the Christian religion itself is based on duality. It was fashioned by men who were familiar with Christ's words, but for the most part did not share his experience of unity consciousness.

The governing powers of early Christendom decided that man is separate from God and can find salvation only through accepting Christ as his savior—and only then through the agency of a priest and the church. I have no doubt they did this so the church could reign supreme and exert greater control over people's lives. So, in the dualistic interpretation of Christ's teaching, your neighbor is separate from you, but if you can love him as you love yourself, then there will be more peace on earth, and you will have fulfilled one of the requirements for salvation.

The Upanishad teaching, on the other hand, is a profoundly nondual statement. It is saying that you and God—*That*—are one. You and the divine energy, the consciousness behind creation, are one. It's the wave and the ocean again.

Huxley pointed to this intersection between Christ's *bhakti*, or heart injunction, and the *jnana*, or wisdom statement from the Upanishads. He said: "Love your neighbor because he *is* yourself."

To see and understand this with the whole of your being, you have to see it from the perspective of consciousness, the vastness of your true nature. This is why I say there is something more important than love. That something is consciousness itself. After all, without consciousness, what is love? Without consciousness, love is always conditional. It is not pure. It is emotional. It has an agenda behind it. It can turn to coldness, dislike, even hate.

But with the light of consciousness and timeless awareness behind it, love is always unconditional. Look at everything in life, then, from the Whole, rather than from the parts. Get the big picture. Take the unconditional perspective, and your love will be unconditional.

Or, as Kunihiro Yamate puts it: "The secret of this way is to look at everything from the perspective of ourselves as pure

Consciousness. It is the only real, true way to look at things."

Love Your Energies

A woman said to me once: "My husband complains I am too emotional because I feel things deeply, especially other people's suffering and the pain of the world. It is easy for me to be moved to tears by what I feel, and then I judge myself for being weepy, overly emotional. Sometimes I will get angry at the injustice of the world and then angry at my husband for judging me. How do I find the balance with my own emotional energy without becoming like my husband, who lives in his head and who seems so detached from his emotions?"

One of the main barriers to freedom is the conflict we often experience with our feeling, emotional self. Like the woman's husband, whenever we live too much in our heads, whenever we repress any feeling, be it sadness, anger, fear, or even love, it eats away inside us. Over the long term, it can damage both our psyche and our health.

Many a case of high blood pressure, stomach ulcers, irritable bowel syndrome, or diabetes has its origins in the inability or reluctance to own our feelings and emotions. Men, who often tend to be more distant from their emotions than women, need to be aware of this. The fact is it is healthy to feel deeply and be emotionally vulnerable. Feelings, emotions, and even the energy of desire, are just part of what it means to be human. The more you awaken to freedom, the more these energies naturally come into balance and are therefore much less problematic.

In this regard, there is a story about a Zen master who was sitting on a rock, weeping profusely. His student came to him and said, "Master, you're crying! I don't understand. You're enlightened. I thought you were beyond tears."

"Nonsense," the master sniffled. "My oldest friend just died, and naturally I am sad."

A few years after my own spiritual journey began, I went through my first divorce. One day my ex-wife, Briar, brought a friend with her when she came to visit. We were sitting having tea and talking, and as I looked at Briar, I started to think about what went wrong in our marriage. Before I knew it, I began to feel a great sadness inside me. Then tears started to well up. Not wanting to embarrass myself in front of my ex or her friend, I excused myself and went down the hall into the bathroom.

There I let the tears flow, all the pent-up emotion of my divorce, all the unresolved feelings I was still struggling with inside. Remember, I was fairly new to my spiritual journey and dealing with all kinds of inner demons. I didn't know myself very well at all.

Anyway, as I looked at myself in the bathroom mirror, tears streaming down my face, I noticed a small card pinned to the wall next to the mirror. It was a saying of Jesus that I had put there, and I read the words: "Love your energies."

I remember blinking, unsure whether I read correctly or not. Surely Jesus hadn't said those words. I blinked again, wiped the tears from my eyes, and looked at the card more closely. Sure enough, it said: "Love your *enemies*."

But the real message was not lost on me. As far as I was concerned, it was a sign from the universe, and my first reading—"Love your energies"—was the real meaning behind Jesus' words.

After all, it is the enemy we perceive living within us, our own demons, conflicted feelings, and turbulent emotions—in short, our *energies*—that we must first love, else how can we begin to love those people whom we do perceive as our enemies? How can we truly love another if we can't love ourselves first?

I remember smiling through my tears and saying to myself: "Hey, my sadness is one of my energies, and so is any embarrassment I might feel around being sad. It's time to start loving these energies, Jim." With that, I went back into the living room to join Briar and her friend and to share my feelings and my insight with them.

A friend once said to me he thought the spiritual journey was all about acceptance, and that it was the serene acceptance of whatever is happening that paves the way for unconditional love. This is an accurate insight. The more you learn to dwell in acceptance the less you resist life and the less suffering you experience. Awakening, or inner freedom, is to live in total acceptance of life. To flow with it.

The more you are able to embrace, welcome, and accept each experience which happens in your life as a gift, the closer you move to true freedom. This does not mean you let the people in your life take advantage of you. Nor does it mean you don't act to bring about changes in unwanted experiences or you don't seek to improve your lot in life.

By learning this *inward* acceptance of what is, you no longer put up resistance. Without resistance there can be no conflict or suffering. Your heart opens more and you see everything more clearly, which means you take the most intelligent, creative, and loving action...

Practice inner acceptance now... Go within and connect with the spaciousness inside you... Breathe, and feel the energy and warmth of your heart... Notice if there is any story active in your mind causing stress or tension in you... See if you can just be with it, accept it, the way it is... You can quietly affirm to yourself, "I am not my story, I am the pure awareness present right now..." Then be the awareness looking through your eyes... You are just flowing with the moment, allowing the whole of life to wash through you... Everything you see, feel, hear, taste... You are open to all of it, resisting nothing, because you realize at an intuitive level, acceptance is the doorway to true inner freedom...

Don't Take Your Emotions Personally

People can feel overwhelmed by their emotions. Sometimes being overwhelmed is what needs to happen. It is important to notice that the feelings and emotions come in waves.

If you are being overtaken by a wave of emotion, there is really nothing to do but let it happen. At the same time, be very aware of everything you are feeling. Whether you label it as "fear," "anger," "sadness," or some other emotion, don't get lost in a story about it. Stay present with the feeling, and allow it to unfold, to have its expression.

In Chapter One I spoke of the two contributions Jean Klein made to my spiritual understanding. One was the idea of welcoming whatever was happening. The other was stepping back with my awareness. This helped by giving me the capacity to be fully *in* an experience, and at the same time be detached from it, to be aware *of* the experience.

I did not include the stepping-back process in the three-step practice because many seekers could not successfully visualize it, or had difficulty doing it. Fortunately, it is not essential for awakening. What *is* essential is not resisting your suffering, noticing the story you are telling yourself, and being very present with your whole energy. And then seeing you are *not* the story, but rather what is looking at the story, as well as everything else.

Nevertheless, I had my first taste of this stepping-back aspect of Jean's teaching when I was in a marriage counseling session. It was concerning my impending divorce, my second, from my son's mother. I was feeling a lot of pain around the break-up of our little family, yet I knew it needed to happen because of the irreconcilable differences between us.

I was sitting on the couch in the therapist's office and started to weep. Then suddenly I remembered Jean's teaching. I sat up and positioned my awareness slightly behind and above myself. I was present as the witness of what I was experiencing. A remarkable thing happened. I was able to feel the sadness and watch the tears, and just let them flow without any judgment, without being caught up in them. I felt the grief, but wasn't lost in it.

It was an extraordinarily transforming moment. Thereafter, whenever I felt any emotion I was able to experience it fully and honestly, and yet some part of me was always free of it. Some part of me was always in pure awareness, the witness of what was happening.

It was then I discovered that no matter what was happening in this body/mind, I—as awareness, as consciousness—was bigger than it. I was bigger than whatever I was experiencing.

The key is allowing everything to arise, especially your emotions. Let the waves of feeling come when they come. Don't try to resist or get caught up in thinking, analyzing, judging, or trying to understand what is happening. Just stay present and be very aware. Notice if there are sensations in different parts of your body as the emotions ebb and flow. If it starts to get overwhelming, remind yourself: "This too shall pass."

The understanding always comes later, when the waves of intense feeling or emotion subside. The more you allow yourself to just experience whatever you're experiencing, staying completely present in the here and now with your awareness, the more the meaning of those experiences will be revealed. Perhaps you already know what I am talking about. Sometimes a situation is confusing, and not till much later does insight dawn.

What becomes clear on this path of awakening is the more you hold onto the need to have things be a certain way, the more you insist *this* isn't right, or *that* should not be allowed, the more emotional charge you are storing up.

Then, when expectations are not met, there is pain and suffering. If your position is exposed as being hollow or false, you might experience sadness or embarrassment. If someone belittles you, puts you down in some way, or betrays you it may express as resentment or anger.

So the work is to welcome, or at least accept your suffering, and then look at what you are inwardly holding onto, the beliefs, expectations, pictures, and ideas. Look at the story you are telling yourself about who you are and what you need to be happy. Begin to see that it is only a story, a story you are making up. It is a story entirely of your own creation.

Realize you are not the story, but the luminous ever-present consciousness which looks at the story, which *creates* the story, and you'll have a genuine experience, a taste, of freedom.

After all, the story you tell yourself keeps the emotions in a volatile state of readiness. As I said, when you cling to any point of view or psychological position, you are generating an emotional charge.

Freedom comes as you see the story for what it is: a figment of your own creation. When you're not holding onto any idea or image of yourself, there's no build-up of emotional energy. You are simply open to life in the present. The secret is in emphasizing *awareness* itself, having all your senses alert, and not getting lost in thinking. Then your head will be clear, and you will feel the deeper energy, the deeper beauty and power of creation itself, and it will nourish you. Then your emotions will come into balance. They will arise spontaneously and authentically.

You will feel sadness at the loss of a loved one, or perhaps in a moment of being confronted with the tremendous suffering of so many innocent people in our world. Or you might feel anger whenever you are reminded of the terrible injustices still taking place, the brutality, the subjugation of one group of people by another.

But none of these feelings will be taken too personally. The "I" won't jump in and make some new kind of story out of them, such as a victim story, as in, "Woe is me, the world is too awful and I am too sensitive to live in it." People who really believe they are victims are always telling their tale of suffering to anyone who will listen, and this constant reinforcement of their story just keeps them stuck.

As you grasp this teaching and let go of the attachment to and identification with your own story, you begin to know yourself as awareness, the pure consciousness behind everything. You start to free yourself. Emotions still arise and pass, but now they happen more spontaneously. The paradox of awakening or enlightenment is that while you feel very deeply, you don't take your feelings personally. Once you let go of the identification with your own story, you learn to let go of the attachment to other peoples' stories as well.

Then, in the clarity of your true nature, you see what action, if any, needs to be taken. If something needs to be done about the situation triggering the emotional response, you'll know what to do, and you'll do it. But you won't make a big drama out of it.

Now, if you choose to be involved in an intimate relationship, as most of us do, then, no matter how awake and free you are, your feelings are always going to be somewhat at risk. If you experience rejection, abandonment, or betrayal from a person you love, you will certainly feel some kind of a sting, and it may even last a while. Perhaps there is some lesson to be learned from the experience.

But know this: if your awakening is genuine, deep down you will still be at peace within. The peace never goes away.

In this regard, I am reminded of a Zen saying: "Now that my house has burned to the ground, I have an unobstructed view of the rising moon."

This is one of the most exquisite teachings on what it means to be inwardly free. You don't want your house to burn down (or your relationship to end) and if it's on fire, you do everything you can to save it. If your house does burn down, you will naturally grieve the loss. But then, at some point, you look up above the smoking ruins, and there—lo!—the huge, pale silver orb of the moon becomes visible, creeping slowly up into the night sky.

What a magnificent sight! Ah, such beauty, such beauty which is always here, even in the midst of sorrow.

The Relationship Mirror

A woman asked me this question about her relationship:

"My boyfriend is often arrogant and controlling. It seems he always needs to be right. I have been with him for two years. The only reason why I stay is that he also has a sweet, tender side to him. How can I bring more of the sweetness out in him, and less of the arrogance?"

If you are a parent, and care about conscious parenting you learn early on never to disapprove of your child, only of their behavior. It is the same with other people including this woman's boyfriend. His *behavior* is the problem. True, someone may exhibit arrogant behavior so frequently it seems they are the very embodiment of arrogance. But on the journey of awakening we are always looking for the deeper beauty in people, the interconnectedness that is our common thread.

Underneath the mask of arrogance you will find an insecure human being. And beneath the insecurity is the vastness, the beauty, the freedom of the person's true spiritual nature. Of course, he (for arrogance is usually a male problem) is disconnected from that truth. But the less you judge him for his arrogance, and the more able you are to relate to him in an open, friendly, non-threatening way, the more likely he is to soften and see himself and his behavior more realistically.

However, here's something very useful to know: if another person's arrogance, resentment, anger, or confusion is a problem for you, it is a good time to ask yourself: "So, where does this emotion or state—whether it be arrogance, resentment, anger, confusion, or something else I dislike in the other person—exist in me?"

I call this the "relationship mirror." When we see something in someone else we find offensive or annoying it is often because the same or similar trait exists within us. By focusing on judging the other person for it, we get to avoid looking at our own emotional patterns. We project out onto others what we don't wish to see in ourselves.

If you are experiencing conflict, anxiety, or suffering in a relationship, it's your clue that something is going on inside you which needs looking at. Again, simply say: "I welcome, or at least accept, this experience... It is showing me where I am not yet free."

The woman who asked about her boyfriend had, in fact, a subtle judgment toward him. I said to her: "The act of judging your boyfriend, which in itself is a kind of arrogance, creates suffering within you. You feel a certain tension when you are around him; you have this withheld energy toward him. You're holding up a barrier between you and him. You can't be open or authentic with him, perhaps because of your timidity.

"When you live like this, judging and distancing yourself from him, you may not feel like you are suffering, but by holding onto a fixed judgment, position, or point of view, it means there is resistance to the natural flow of communication. You can't be completely present and honest with him or yourself. Whenever there is a lack of authenticity in your life, the seeds of suffering are already germinating."

Then she responded by saying: "Couldn't the other person be at fault, though? If I am with someone—even someone other than my boyfriend—who is mean, who is unkind, even abusive, wouldn't it be natural to feel resentful?"

"Resentment is not natural," I replied. "It is a conditioned response. Conditioned, again, by the culturally and socially reinforced belief about happiness lying outside us, and to be happy—i.e. not suffer internally in any way—the other person must exhibit at least a modicum of kindness and civility.

"Let's be clear here. This entire work we are exploring is about *your* freedom, *your* awakening. The freer you become, the less you will be at the effect of other peoples' stuck, reactive, unconscious patterns of behavior. Then you will be able to influence, guide, and lead others to freedom."

In other words, you could be having lunch with the angriest person in the world, and while the intensity of their energy may make you choose to not sit too close to them, you will not take any of their words or behaviors personally. Because you know yourself, and are genuinely relaxed and at peace within, you will not be providing any resistance to this other person's anger.

I was in a workshop once when the teacher gave us a

wonderful phrase designed to immediately defuse relationship tension: "This doesn't mean anything about me." When someone starts attacking, accusing, or blaming you in some way, if you find yourself taking it personally, say to yourself, "This doesn't mean anything about me."

Even though the other person may be convinced the problem is all because of you, they are just acting out their own inner suffering and projecting it all onto you. There may be an element of truth in what they are saying, so you can take the feedback and put it to good use. Apply it towards improving your communication skills or becoming a better human being.

When being given feedback about my own behavior, I did not always like what I was hearing, but I have grown a lot through my willingness to listen to it. Above all, don't start judging yourself just because others may be judging you. Listen carefully for the truth, but don't give undue meaning or weight to another's words or opinions. Don't believe their story around you.

When you stop taking the other person's criticism personally, when you no longer judge them or make them wrong, they will find being around you disarming. They are more likely to feel accepted and heard by you. Their anger will have nowhere to land. It will pass right by you. In that kind of non-threatening openness, people are more liable to see themselves, their anger, or their arrogance more clearly. They may even experience a healing or transformation.

But to come back to the point I was making a short while ago, here is the key to seeing what is true for you in terms of your inner emotional reality: any feelings or emotions you may be repressing, or not acknowledging, constitute suffering. If any situation or any person causes conflict or upset in you, ask yourself the kinds of questions which will lead you to the insight you seek, such as:

"So, what is going on with me?"

"Why am I am reacting this way?"

"What is it I need to look at it in myself?"

At the same time you ask yourself those questions, remember

to say to yourself, "Ah, I welcome this situation, or this feeling, because it is showing me where I am not yet free."

Then be silent. Be quiet, be still. Listen inwardly for whatever comes up, whether new feelings, new insights, or something else. The secret of communication, both with yourself and with others, is silence. The deeper your silence, the clearer your thinking and the more potent your words. The willingness to be quietly, alertly present as you accept and embrace your own discomfort is the true doorway to freedom.

As I have said before, the insight into your own emotional state may not come immediately. But just by living with the question, "What is causing this unhappiness within me?" sooner or later the answer will be revealed to you. It may appear in the form of some old story or some memory you still identify with. The moment you simultaneously realize you are *not* the story, not the memory, but you are the lucid ever-present awareness noticing the story, you will be free.

The proof that freedom is becoming more real for you will again show up in the relationship mirror. You will notice other people's insecurities, fears, and even the psychological and emotional games they play, but you will see past all that. You will see what they themselves do not see.

You will see into the truth of their being, the beauty at their core. You will see an expression of divine consciousness, the same consciousness manifesting through your body, mind, and self. Recognizing and honoring this is the essence of love.

In Zen, it is spoken of as the "empty mirror." It's one of the signs of enlightenment. You look into a mirror, and there's no one there. There's just the light and beauty of clear radiant consciousness shining back at you through two wide-open eyes.

Raising Children with Love

The more consciously and lovingly we raise our children, the less psychological and emotional baggage they grow up with, and the freer they are. However, our children still have their own karma, their own issues to work out. They need to find things out for themselves.

As the father of a son who is now a young man, one of the most important things I learned about raising children was also from Jean Klein. He said we love most those around whom we feel the freest to be ourselves. Meditate on this saying for a moment. Think of how it applies in your own life.

Isn't it true that the friends you value the most are the ones who give you the most space to be yourself, who truly accept you for who you are, and even when you act like a jerk, they still love you?

The main thing as a parent is not to become attached to the image of "father" or "mother." For example, be a father when the father role is necessary. But don't get hung up on the "father knows best" dynamic in the way many fathers do, as if the father is somehow superior to the son or daughter.

Instead, just be there just as a kind, loving, tremendously caring friend or ally. Give your children guidance when needed. Enter and learn about their world when invited. Provide a focus or direction for their energy until they are able to do it for themselves. Establish firm boundaries when they are needed.

I always gave my son a lot of freedom to explore and discover life for himself. Looking back from this perspective, I probably gave him too much freedom. If I were doing it again today, I would be more hands-on, more present as a guide for him. At the time though, I was caught up in my own journey of self-discovery.

Nevertheless, I tried to make sure he understood that freedom and responsibility go hand-in-hand. I let him know that I would give him as much freedom as he was willing to be responsible for. It happened very rarely, but once in a while when he was young I had to discipline him. For example I let him know that I had certain expectations about his level of performance at school.

When I once mentioned this to a friend, he said to me, "I thought awakening was about being free of expectations?"

Even with awakening you can still have certain expectations, but you're just not *attached* to them, I replied. In other words, if my son doesn't fulfill the few but important expectations I have of him, it is not going to disturb my inner peace or well-being.

My expectations of him are really for him, not for me. As a parent, as someone who has been around the block many times, I know how the world works. It is demanding and competitive. Generally, the strong and educated flourish while the weak and uneducated barely survive. As a parent, naturally I want my son to flourish, especially from within—to feel strong and confident, both in his inner being and in his ability to focus on and accomplish his goals in life. Most parents want this for their children.

So, when playing the role of father or mother, and when laying down certain rules, it may be necessary to be firm. But where the letting go comes in, where the consciousness becomes evident, is that it is all done without being emotionally attached to outcomes. You give your best to your children, but ultimately what happens is out of your hands.

A wise person once told me you are responsible for your efforts, not the results. You set your intention to ensure the best possible outcome, but you keep your attention right here, fully in the present.

One area where strong residues can arise from time-to-time (it was the only "real" residue I had) is around our kids. We are biologically, genetically, and emotionally connected to our children, so it is inevitable that we are going to be concerned about their well-being, and maybe even suffer a little, because of that concern. Just to be aware of that, to notice when we are getting caught up in a story around them, is liberating.

Do that in your parenting, and your kids will love being around you. You will have a special, unique, truly beautiful relationship which will last a lifetime. Sounds good, doesn't it?

So, let's take a minute to breathe, relax, and simply accept, even welcome, whatever is. Feel into the silence, the love, the beauty that is here right now, all around us. The best and most creative actions always flow out of this clear sense of *being*.

Whether it is parenting, exercising, making money, or indulging in the sheer joy of creating, these activities flow effortlessly when we are fully established in the present moment.

Let's be here now.

A Practice For Connecting With Another Person

The most accurate gauge or proof of how present and inwardly free we are is in our ability to connect with other people without fear, in a relaxed, non-threatening way. Our look is open and welcoming. We have nothing to hide or prove.

I use the following practice in my workshops. It can bring up our fears, anxieties, discomforts, judgments, etc., particularly when we are meeting someone for the first time. This allows us to see how much "stuff" is getting in the way of our connecting genuinely with others. It can trigger the stories we are still internally identifying with.

However, the ultimate purpose of this practice is to give us the practical experience of being with others in a relaxed, open, non-judgmental, and loving way.

Sit facing your partner (or a friend), close enough so your knees are touching. Then each of you close your eyes, and establish a sense of calmness and spaciousness by simply welcoming everything— your body, the sensations, feelings, breath, arising thoughts, beliefs, stories…

When you feel sufficiently relaxed and clear, open your eyes and look at your partner. Let your eyes be soft, open, and receptive, as if you are inviting the whole world to come to you. Gently hold each other's gaze for a period of five minutes the first couple of times, then longer, maybe up to ten minutes, as you get more used to it.

While doing the practice, pay attention to any judgmental thoughts arising, whether about yourself or your partner. Above all, don't judge yourself for being judgmental; don't criticize yourself for being critical. If you notice this happening, just breathe, then tell yourself: "Uh-oh, I'm doing it again—getting caught up in a story," and come back to being present with your partner.

See the beauty and light in their eyes. Recognize that what you see in them is a perfect mirror of your own beauty and light. After all, there is just one beautiful, radiant consciousness here, embodied in two separate people.

This can, especially early on, be an intense process. If you need to periodically close your eyes and re-center, give yourself total permission to do so. Then, when you are ready, come back to gazing in your partner's eyes. When you and your partner feel like you've spent enough time connecting in this way, give each other a warm hug and share your personal experience of the practice.

Chapter Seven

Creating A New Story For Your Life

Others before me have stated we are not our stories, so the teaching in this book is not new. Advaita itself, which dates back to Shankara in the 8th century, teaches we are not the person we think we are.

However, this book combines the teaching and practice in a unique and new way, potent and relevant to our age. It blends the spiritual and material into one dynamic, unified or nondual whole. Its essential message is that life is happening right here, right now, and what has previously been considered "spiritual" *is* the "material," and vice-versa. It is all one reality, and we human beings are manifestations of this reality. It matters not what we may be or do in some as yet unknown future. It is how we are *being*, and what we *do* right now which matters.

A different way of stating the teaching is this: Everything which can be seen changes, but you are the *seeing*, which never changes. Know yourself as the seeing, and you'll always be fulfilled, at peace, and in the flow of life. You'll always be on purpose with your own unique mission or destiny here.

Let me explain in more depth. First, everything which can be seen changes. This becomes obvious the more closely you look at it. Our bodies change. They mature, age, and eventually die. Our thoughts, beliefs, sensations, and feelings change all the time. Our *stories* change. Even a devout religious story, whether about God or some other power, changes. It comes and goes, grows weaker or stronger over time, and is subject to vast numbers of interpretations. Then, of course, our friends and relationships change as they, too, come and go. And the world around us, both natural and man-made, is always changing.

The second key phrase of the teaching says you are the *seeing*, that which never changes. Think about it. Who or what in you is reading these words, words which themselves are changing, moving past your eyes as you read? You may say: "Well, *I* am." But then who is this "I?" Can you actually find the "I" anywhere in your mind, in your consciousness? Or is this "I," too, just a concept, the story-*teller*, an object in consciousness just as elusive as any other object or concept?

You definitely have a sense of unique individuality. You know "you" exist. But when you look within and try to find this "you" which you take yourself to be, you won't be able to find it. Anything you say about yourself, no matter how "true" it may seem to be, will be just another concept—another story. And, as we have seen, all stories, no matter how true they seem to be, can be observed, or seen—and, as a result, they change.

So again I ask: who or what in you *sees* the ever-changing stories you tell yourself?

This is the essential question, and many of you reading this have at least a taste of the answer, which of course is not found in words, but only in *being*. One taste of the freedom, joy, and spaciousness of your true nature is all it really takes to orient you, to point you toward Home. And the three-step practice we have been doing throughout this journey together helps you establish the sense of being Home.

What you are, then, is the *seeing*. You are pure, universal consciousness, the awareness looking out through your eyes. This seeing, in concert with all the other senses, perceives the unfolding reality of your life as it is happening right now.

For those of you who may still be struggling with this, just comprehending it intellectually is a good start. To understand you are not your story, that everything that can be seen changes, and you are the seeing, which never changes, is a big step. Living with this understanding and contemplating it daily helps bring it into the cells of your body, so that it gradually becomes your actual, felt experience.

The third key phrase of the message above is that once you know yourself as the seeing, you are free. This is the "fourth" step I have talked about: seeing through the illusion of the "I," the "me," the ego itself. Once you've made the shift from identifying yourself with your stories to recognizing your true identity as the unchanging consciousness looking through your eyes and giving rise to all the stories in your life, including the ego or story-teller itself, then you will be fulfilled and at peace with yourself.

When you know yourself as consciousness, you are in touch with the source of manifestation. Just being the consciousness you already are, tends to bring forth whatever you focus on, whatever you truly need or want. And while thoughts themselves are unreal, in the sense you can't actually find them anywhere, they do serve a purpose. You use them for communication and creativity, for making good decisions, and for manifesting your goals or intentions in physical reality.

After all, everything man-made, from the biggest sky-scrapers to the tiniest microchips, from forms of government to programs for feeding the poor, began with a thought, an idea, or a picture in someone's mind. So, be clear about your intentions. Be clear about what you want. Contemplate your purpose, goals, and objectives several times a day and then forget about them. Come back to the power of the present, and enjoy the flow of whatever you happen to be experiencing, whatever happens to be manifesting in this moment.

Now, a question that arises from time to time is this: "Some people have told me that awakening or enlightenment is a process where we get freer and freer, but because we are human, there will always be some degree of suffering. However, you seem to be saying once we awaken, we are free, and there is no more suffering at the personal level. What is the truth here?"

My answer is this: once awakening happens, then it has

happened. There is no going back. You don't get lost in separation again, although there will be times when those residues of past suffering may flare-up and cause you to momentarily seem to "forget" your true nature.

However, the belief that it is a process is quite common. Perhaps this is because while we are still seeking, there is definitely a feeling of getting freer year by year. Some people assume the seeker just keeps going through different doors into greater levels of freedom, but there is still this "you" experiencing these different levels.

This is where a guide, teacher, or someone who has actually gone through the last door can make a big difference. The guide holds up a mirror, metaphorically speaking, so the seeker can see him or herself, and reality, more clearly. A Zen story illustrates how such a mirror can set someone free.

Keiji, a long-time student of Zen, came to his master and said: "I don't see how there can be any enlightenment setting you free once and for all. I think we just get ever greater glimpses of Buddha-nature, the vastness that is our true Being. It's an ever-expanding process."

"That may be what you think," the master replied, giving Keiji a fierce look. "But what is your experience? Your experience right *now*?"

Keiji looked momentarily confused. "My experience right now, Master?"

"Yes. Do you know yourself as Keiji, having ever-expanding experiences of Buddha-nature? Or do you know yourself as Buddha-nature, having the experience of Keiji?"

When the master said this, it was as if a switch tripped in Keiji's mind. Light suddenly flooded his consciousness. Gone were all his concepts and ideas. A huge smile lit up his face as he realized at last that he wasn't Keiji, but that he was Buddha-nature having the experience of Keiji—and that everyone and everything was, in their essence, Buddha-nature. In this way he finally discovered the enlightenment he was seeking.

Imagination And Positive Thinking

What are your goals and dreams, what is the vision you have for your life? How do you want to serve?

Dr. Albert Schweitzer, the great humanitarian and Nobel Prize winner, made this statement when he addressed a group of young people after the Second World War: "I don't know what your destiny will be, but one thing I do know: the only ones among you who will truly be happy are those who have sought and found how to serve."

These are true and powerful words, as inspiring today as when he first spoke them. Once awakening happens, life becomes rich in love, meaning, and purpose. Awakening liberates you from self-concern, from self-obsession, from images and ideas of "self," period. You don't take anything personally because you no longer hold onto any idea or image of yourself as some kind of a "person." Instead, you view everything from the perspective of pure consciousness. You see what needs to be done in any given moment, and you take action and do it. You see how you want to serve, how you are guided to serve from awareness, not from ego or personal agenda.

You feel moved to write a new, *conscious* story for your life. One of the joys of awakening is you finally get clear about what you are here to do, what identity you now want to consciously assume in the marketplace of daily life. And it is different for every one of us. Some, like me, become teachers, guides, way-showers. Others volunteer, or make their contribution in the arts, business, a profession, trade, or in public or private life. The creative possibilities are endless. It doesn't matter what you do, just that you do it.

Now, imagination is a powerful function of the mind. It is the ability to form images, and to visualize concepts and pictures of desired results. Imagination is the art of dreaming up new realities and consciously creating what you want.

Like intuition, reason, and logic, imagination is one of the mental tools we have available to help solve problems. With this mental paintbrush, you can do many things: visualize potential outcomes, picture whole scenarios, and play with possible solutions. Or, perhaps you are feeling called to do something different, something more creative with your life. You can use your imagination to envision new possibilities. You can let your imagination run wild. It's fun to do this, to play around in your mind. Maybe you are making love with your partner, and want to explore new ways to please each other. Use your imagination. That's what it's there for.

The thing to remember, as Jean Klein said once, is that imagination is meant to enhance living, not substitute for it.

I was asked this question once: "What about fantasies, whether it's a sexual fantasy, dreaming about the perfect relationship or job, being rich and famous, or whatever?"

A fantasy is really just an exaggerated feel-good story. The problem with fantasies is they don't go anywhere. They don't produce anything. But, if you tend to fantasize a lot, there is a way you can honor your mind's tendency and still rein it in. I know this works because my mind frequently got caught in fantasies.

Here's the technique: allow yourself to indulge in a particular fantasy, any fantasy, for one minute and then drop it. Come back to being very aware or conscious in the present. Come back to this moment now, to what you are sensing, feeling, perceiving now. Then, if you feel the need to revisit the fantasy, pick it up, but again only for one minute. Engage the fantasy as many times as you like during the day, but only for one minute at a time.

This technique literally "starves" the fantasy. You begin to lose interest in it. Soon, you are doing it for only thirty seconds, and then ten or fifteen seconds. Very quickly you start becoming more interested in the power and vitality of your actual living experience, what you are sensing and feeling right here, right now.

Don't forget, if you are using fantasy or imagination to reinforce your ego's insecurities, then your mind has you in its grip, in its story. Our goal here is to turn it around and to become free of our mind, the net of thought. Only then can we dwell effortlessly in clear present-time awareness, in what Zen refers to as empty mind or no-mind.

You'll experience an extraordinary feeling of openness and spaciousness inside you when you finally see you are not your thoughts, but rather you are the consciousness which gives rise to those thoughts. There will be no "you" in the way, no self-concept, no self-image obstructing the flow of life and creative energy. You'll know yourself as the universe, the ocean of universal consciousness, expressing through this body/mind, through this wave form you are.

Then thoughts will no longer be a problem. They will come and go as before, but you won't identify yourself with them. Your mind generates thoughts and stories, but when awakened, those thoughts emerge from awareness and you can take delight in freely using them to create all sorts of things. Since your mind is no longer a source of stress or anxiety, you can have a blast dancing around in it, playing with the images and ideas.

Once you are free of the addiction to fantasies, guess what? You can indulge them on occasion. A little fantasy once in a while is okay.

Take time to practice indulging a fantasy, then letting it go, right now... Go into your mind and consciously engage a favorite fantasy... Really dramatize it, picture it vividly, in your mind. Feel the feelings it evokes in your body. Play with it... Then, just as consciously, let it go and simply be here... Know you have a mind which generates thoughts, stories, and fantasies... You have a body with feelings, emotions, and sensations... And you have a personality with qualities, quirks, and foibles... But who and what you really are is vastly bigger than anything you can see or experience... So relax, breathe, and be the awareness you are...

Another question I get is: "What about addictions? I mean to smoking, drinking, drugs, food, and so on? How best to deal with them?"

When facing addictions, you've got to really watch for the story you're telling yourself as you're about to reach for the object of your addiction, whether it's a cigarette, a drink, food, or whatever. Maybe you say: "I deserve this treat," or "A drink will help settle me down." Then see that it is just a story. It is not your true nature. It is not pure consciousness.

Telling yourself a new story about the negative consequences of your addictive behavior can be helpful and potentially healing, but it is only a stepping stone because it is still a story. The main thing is, if you are going to indulge in the addiction, do it very *consciously*. Don't get lost in yet another story, such as "I'll quit tomorrow." Be completely conscious and present even as you give in to the addiction.

A good practice to do as you are learning to be more conscious about your addictions is to pause for a moment before reaching for that cigarette, food, drink, or drug, and ask yourself a simple question: "Do I really want this right now?" Then listen carefully for the answer from deep within.

When you realize that the addiction is a way of numbing yourself out, of rendering you even *more* unconscious, then gradually you'll wean yourself from it. Or rather, it will leave you. As Jean Klein said once, "Things leave us when they no longer fulfill their promise."

People sometimes ask me about the value of positive thinking. On another occasion, Jean said: "If you are going to think, it is better to think positively than negatively."

The limitation of negative thinking is obvious: stressful, anxiety-producing thoughts like "Oh, my God, everything seems so hopeless!" or "I just can't take this anymore!" result in feelings of unhappiness and depression.

The limitation of positive thinking is not so obvious, because positive thoughts, such as "I *can* succeed at this," or "I feel wonderfully clear and relaxed inside," have a correspondingly positive effect on the psyche. They fill us with optimism. They can make us feel good. They give us a lift.

Yet what is the motive behind adopting positive thinking as a way of being? Invariably, it is to support and reinforce the ego's desire for meaning and security. This need is based on the belief that, if I just think positively, good things will happen to me, my life will improve, and I will be a happy human being.

It is coming from the old paradigm of *do, have, be,* where you are still looking outside yourself for fulfillment. *Do* this first—think and act positively—and you will *have* the circumstances allowing you to *be* happy. The problem is your inner peace and happiness are then dependent upon what you have and thus they are always conditional.

The awakened paradigm for living is characterized by the rule of "*be* first, and then *do,* so you can *have.*" You learn to *be* at peace within yourself through the three-step practice, and through understanding the teaching that you are not your thoughts or your story. The more you do the practice and remember the teaching, the more you are at peace, regardless of what is going on outside with other people, or your life situation.

Lao Tzu said, in the *Tao Te Ching*: "The way to do is to be." Authentic action, *doing,* flows naturally out of being. Then, out of being content and at ease in the present, you not only do what you love to do, but what you feel called to do, or whatever needs to be done.

Awakened or not, what you do results in *having* certain outcomes manifest—the fruits of your actions, whether in relationships, work, health, recreation, or finances. The big difference with awakening is, since you already *are* at peace within and not dependent on these things for inner peace and well-being, you will be able to fully enjoy the results. The outer gifts are like a bonus, icing on the proverbial cake of life.

However, in answer to the question about positive thinking, affirming the statement "To be awake and conscious is my natural state of being" is definitely more helpful than saying "Life sucks" and then feeling hopeless.

But the awakening to inner freedom is our natural, felt state of *being*. We didn't create it. It already and always *is*. To truly discover it, the mind must be free of *all* thought, especially the "I" or "me" thought. Our true, awakened nature is discovered here, *now*.

Manifestation

A man opened up in a workshop, and said this: "I was once very financially successful. I knew how to set goals and achieve them, to manifest things in material reality. Yet the truth was I wasn't happy. Then, some years ago, a tragedy happened in my life which caused me to re-evaluate everything. It started me on the spiritual path.

"I began meditating, reading spiritual books, going to workshops, and learning about living in the present, as you say. I am definitely more at peace now, but I seem to have lost the power—or maybe it is the interest—to make things happen in my life. Now I struggle financially in a way I never used to. What is going on?"

Many people who embark upon the spiritual quest grapple with the issue of success. What happens now to the worldly goals and desires they once had? What about their desire to accomplish something in life, or to leave a mark of some kind? Very often, when people turn their attention inwards, it seems they lose their ability to manifest outer results, whether it be a career goal or the money needed to live a comfortable life, with income consistently exceeding expenses, instead of the other way around.

I remember soon after meeting Jean Klein I met a man, Ted, who was a student of Jean's. One day, Ted invited me back to the house in Marin County where his wife and daughter lived. Ted was in the process of getting a divorce, and while he was in the back talking to his daughter, I spoke to his wife. Picking up one of Jean's books which happened to be lying on the table I asked her, "So, what do you think of this stuff?"

She rolled her eyes. "Well, it's all very interesting, but it doesn't have much to do with real life, does it?"

Her answer didn't surprise me. Ted had already told me one of the reasons they were divorcing was that she didn't support his spiritual practice. For her, true happiness lay in the tangible reality of material objects, not in what she interpreted as ethereal notions of "spiritual freedom." She wanted him to get a high-paying job and earn the kind of income which would allow them to enjoy the finer things in life. Living in Marin was expensive, after all.

As it happens, spiritual awakening is not incompatible with worldly success. Indeed, if it was, few would be interested in it! Fortunately, the same basic principles needed for material success are the same principles needed for awakening. One is focused outwardly, the other is directed inwardly. Once you realize this, then you can find a balance in your life.

If you really want freedom, you must make awakening to your inner being your primary goal. But you can also use the same energies to consciously create what you want in your outer, worldly life. The difference now is that you are not attached to the outcome.

At first, mastering your mind leads to inner peace and freedom, but then you can harness the power of your mind for the purpose of shaping a better world. Ultimately, you come to realize there is no difference between the spiritual and the material. There is just one, divine energy, consciousness, endlessly manifesting in different forms. That's the definition of the term "nondual wisdom" in a nutshell.

Manifestation is actually a very simple process. The more you know yourself as consciousness and live in the knowing, the easier it happens. Sometimes all you have to do is just think of what you want, and before you know it, it shows up.

Just take a few minutes each day to sit down and internally visualize what you want to happen. Or go for a walk, or a run, and do it. But get clear about your intention. The more real you make it, the better. Involve as many senses as you can. You can even say a brief affirmation, as in: "I easily and effortlessly manifest the perfect job right now," or "the perfect relationship end your story. **Begin your life...**

right now."

Actually *see* and *feel* it happening, as if it were already so. This is an important key: to see the thing—what you have intended, what you want—as already having *happened*. On the inside, in your mind and your heart, it is already a vivid reality for you. Now, you are simply waiting to have it show up on the outside.

Then let go of the visualization or affirmation, and any attachment to how it *should* manifest. Completely let go, surrendering the goal or intention to universal will, as you come back to the experience of whatever is happening right now. Then proceed with your day, making sure to focus your energies on any work needing to be done in order to manifest your goal, the thing you want, in reality.

Let's take a closer look at this. First, you must know what you want, whether it is building a successful business, getting in shape physically, finding the perfect mate, or completing some project like writing a book, or mastering creative skills in music or the arts.

You must set your goal or intention. After all, we generally get what we intend. When it comes to being successful in life, intention is everything. So, being very clear about what you want or intend to manifest is critical. Nothing productive can happen without such clarity and inner conviction. Then, as I said above, you must imagine it, see it, as already *so*. The goal or intention is already a living, breathing reality for you on the inside.

Management guru Peter Drucker put it like this: "The best way to predict the future is to create it." You create your future and the results you want, through the clarity and power of your intention.

Second, you have to focus your attention and get passionately engaged in the process. You have to do the work. Sometimes it takes a lot of work to achieve a particular goal, at other times not much at all. The clearer you get inside yourself, the more powerful your ability to manifest.

The key here is *focus*. All successful people, no matter what their area of accomplishment, have sharpened their ability to focus on their goals and intentions. Those who do not succeed at their endeavors tend to be scattered with their energy. They generally lack focus.

Now, for creative, free-ranging thinking it is necessary to be in an expanded state of awareness, which is the exact opposite of focus. There is definitely a time for this kind of inner exploration, for inwardly brainstorming new ideas and possibilities, or just thinking contemplatively about things.

However, in order to actually *make* something happen in the world, you have to contract and focus your energy. You have to pull your energy in. This is how the law of attraction works. Like a magnet, when you pull your energy in, yet are supremely present, you tend to draw what you want to you.

If the process involves work, whether it is a little or a lot, you must totally commit yourself to it. You must throw your body, mind, and heart into it. In order to have anything worthwhile happen in your life, you have to have a passionate desire for it. You have to give energy and attention to it. To find your passion, look inside yourself. Ask yourself what matters to you.

Ask yourself: "If I knew I couldn't fail, what is it I would love to do, what is it I would love to accomplish?"

Many people read, see, or hear about someone else's success and they set out trying to emulate it. They start chasing other people's goals, which never works. Everybody is passionate about something. If you don't already know, keep looking within. Keep trying different things, until you discover what gets your creative juices flowing.

The third part of the process is sometimes the most difficult. It is a theme I have returned to again and again throughout this book. You must now let it go, release all attachment to the outcome. You must surrender; get yourself, your ego, completely out of the way. Realize that everything, ultimately, happens by grace, by a power beyond us, yet expressing through us.

In other words, you set your eyes on the mountaintop, you establish your intention to get there, and then you put it at the back of your mind, and focus on the journey. Without releasing attachment, you just build a new story in your mind and worry, even obsess, about whether you are going to succeed or not. The energy of worry gets in the way of your chances of success.

It's important not to get in your own way and not to get ahead of yourself. What matters is *this* step, the one you are taking right now. Live this moment fully and completely, and the next moment will take care of itself. You will be guided every step of the way. You will intuitively know what to do.

Be Conscious Around Money

I hear this question a lot: "I worry about money constantly—about not being able to pay my bills, about not having enough at the end of the month. How does someone who is awake relate to money?"

For the awakened person, the one who truly knows him or herself, money is just another condition in life, albeit an important one. The awakened person manages his or her capital wisely and usually will not spend more than he or she can afford.

Certainly, as your awakening deepens and matures, you worry less and less about money. As I say in the Appendix, it was one of my residues —the main one, in fact. I was frequently worried about how I was going to pay my bills and meet my financial obligations. But over time, as I embodied my awakening ever more fully, even those worries dropped away. Now, I just make sure to live within my means.

However, money for the unawakened person is nearly always a major issue. Fears around survival, paying the bills, and making it financially cause at least as much stomach distress, if not more, as relationship issues. Money is the number-one issue people fight about in their relationships. In the face of the realities of the marketplace of daily life, it requires nothing less than awakening to be able to let go of worrying about money.

The struggle with money is often an issue for those who

have consciously taken up a spiritual path in life. I've heard statements like this before, and have echoed similar sentiments myself at times in the past:

"Sometimes I think my spirituality is a curse. I look at people I know who don't care about spiritual truths, who just focus on making money. They do well, they get to travel and live in nice homes, and seem pretty happy. Sometimes I think I made the wrong choice in life, and should have just gone for the money, the material prosperity, like most people."

It is true that people who look to money and material security for their happiness usually *are* quite happy—so long as things are going well for them. But it is an inescapable fact: if you are going to make your happiness dependent on outer circumstances, then should those circumstances change, or should you be confronted with even the threat or possibility of change, it will trigger anxiety in you.

It is important to see the whole picture. Those who have no interest in inner freedom, who have put all their faith in the material, in controlling their outer circumstances, experience a very conditional happiness. In our culture, it is easy to be fooled by appearances. The sole mission of the advertising media is to lull us into believing that if we have the purchasing power—i.e. the cash or the credit—to buy lots of beautiful new objects, toys, or services, everything in our life will be rosy.

Obviously, money is a necessary ingredient in a whole and balanced life. You need to take care of your finances in the same way you care for your body, relationships, business, and all areas of your life. However, the more you are tapped into the real source of wealth—the wisdom, love, and creative energy inside you—the more clarity and passion you will bring to your work, and the greater the likelihood of financial success.

You need a vehicle to generate a flow of money, and this is where work comes in. If you do your work well, if you provide real value for those you serve, you will always find people willing to pay for what you have to offer. People will be drawn to your energy and enthusiasm for life, and that itself will bring more outer abundance to you.

Without inner clarity, you will likely be seduced by the promise of happiness coming from something outside of you, the glitz and the glitter. However, no matter how happy people seem, if your happiness is dependent on money, you will live with an undercurrent of anxiety.

A stockbroker friend told me once that she noticed that the more money her clients had, the more they lived in fear of losing it. This is not to say you can't be wealthy and be happy. I am sure there are people who are blessed with wealth, but have also done a lot of inner work, have sought, and maybe even found, the source of peace within themselves.

Money has a vital place in our lives. We all need it to survive, to feed, clothe, house, and educate ourselves and our children. We might need it to care for our elderly parents. We can also enjoy everything else it does for us, like the things it buys us, and the freedom it gives to spend time on purely creative, non money-making pursuits. But when we are in the grip of excessive addiction to it, believing it will save us, or bring us the happiness we seek, we are making a mistake.

The more you face your fears and stories around money, and your real or imagined needs, and realize you are *not* your stories, but rather you are the awareness which *looks* at the stories, the freer you will become of anything binding you.

When I was in my thirties, my own particular fear was of being out of work, out of money, and ending up homeless under a bridge. During my meditations, I faced this worst-case scenario over and over again in my mind, until eventually it no longer held any emotional charge.

I wasn't fully awake yet. I hadn't completely perceived my true nature as consciousness, as the ultimate perceiver, but I came to realize my connection to spirit, the energy behind creation, was strong. I knew how to be at peace in the present and this allowed me to be much freer of my fears around money.

Whether or not I lived under a bridge was certainly not going to take away my inner peace. Besides, there was a whole tradition of Zen masters who lived under bridges, basking in freedom, enjoying the ever-present delights of nature, *dharma-*

jousting with fellow travelers, writing *haiku*. I would have been in good company!

Once I knew this for sure, I then had a clear choice. One option was to sit on my butt meditating in bliss all the time, but with the knowledge I might end up not being able to afford a decent roof over my head. The other was to get to work doing what I enjoyed doing—or at least found tolerable doing—so I could generate the income needed to keep body and soul together in a comfortable way. Preferring middle-class comforts to the deprivation of poverty, I chose the work option.

Remember, the beliefs, images, and pictures in your mind drive the sensations and feelings of anxiety and fear, and keep them alive. As you learn to live in the present, letting go of attachment to the story inside your head, you'll come to the realization that inner freedom is, and always has been, your true nature.

Someone once asked me this question: "As I feel myself drawing ever nearer to the freedom which is my true nature, I notice I want to teach this, to share it, with others. Is it wrong to charge a fee for my services?"

I remember reading an article by the Sufi teacher, Kabir Helminski, many years ago. In it he said: "In Islam, knowledge isn't for sale... There can be no profit motive in sharing the knowledge of illumination; if there is, both sides are being poisoned. A professional class of spiritual advisers does not fit with the truth, and eventually corrupts it."

Unfortunately, this perspective, while honorable in its intent, is the reason why the "spiritual" and the "material" have never merged, and will always be at odds with each other. It maintains and perpetuates the division between the one and the other, and is an ongoing cause of conflict and suffering in people who are caught between their hunger for spiritual truth, and their very real need for material survival.

The nondual or global viewpoint eliminates this division. It sees the spiritual and material as one, unified reality. Thus, it is okay to charge money for the time you may spend delivering the teachings of freedom. After all, money is an essential part of life, and teachers of awakening need to earn a living, too. There needs to be an energy exchange. If the "teacher" is truly free, he or she will not be motivated by greed, and the fee will always be fair, one that the "student" can afford.

The good news, for the "student," is that once he or she awakens to the truth within, no more money needs to be spent. It is an investment which, once made, truly pays dividends, and keeps on paying them, endlessly. The investment results in nothing less than your freedom...

See if you can taste the freedom of your true nature right now... Open up to the inner vastness, the spaciousness, expressing through your body, mind, and personality... Then notice how you have thoughts, beliefs, and stories in your mind, and feelings, emotions, and sensations in your body... Notice how you can observe all these phenomena, so you cannot be them... You are what is observing... You are the timeless, ever-present consciousness witnessing everything arising and falling away in the awareness you are... So, be the awareness... Dwell in the freedom of your true nature...

Lead The Way

A well-dressed man said to me: "I am a senior executive in a Fortune 500 company, and a serious student of the art of leadership. I am extremely busy, have an enormous amount of responsibility, work a minimum of twelve hours a day, and am generally under a lot of pressure. Yet I am interested in what you have to say. I am intrigued by the whole notion of awakening to inner freedom, and how it leads to serving people in a more authentic way. What do you have to say to me?"

Few people will argue against the need for more enlightened

leaders in our world. This man was both a student and practitioner of the art of leadership, so it is good that he was thinking about how to apply these principles and lessons to his work and life.

I told him: "Doubtless you have been inspired by stories of great leadership. You have probably been moved by the example of individuals who embody such qualities as vision, courage, compassion, creative thinking, bold decision-making, and selfless service to humanity. Obviously you want to be the best leader and best person you can possibly be.

"I don't know what specifically motivates you, but I suspect it makes you feel good to be a positive force in helping influence, shape, and direct the creative energy of others. Evidently, you like being of service. No doubt you like being part of a group, team, or organization with good chemistry, one where every member feels a sense of kinship, uniting around a common goal. Experience taught you how to create such unity, and you are clearly willing to take the responsibility for making it happen."

All true leaders understand the power of multiplication, and what can be accomplished when a group of conscious, focused people come together in pursuit of a shared vision. The best leaders use this power not only to produce great results, but to make their organization, their community—and ultimately, our world—a better place.

The greatest leaders in history, from Marcus Aurelius, to Martin Luther King, Jr., to Nelson Mandela, have been the spiritually conscious ones. This has always been the case. The ancient Chinese philosopher, Lao Tzu, spoke about the secret of conscious leadership over two thousand years ago:

"If you want to learn how to govern... Show people the way back to their own true nature."

If, as a leader, you want to be able to bring out the highest and best in others—show them the way back to themselves, as Lao Tzu said—you must achieve a certain level of mastery within yourself, a true meeting of wisdom and love. You don't have to be a saint or completely without ego, but your mind must be clear, your heart open, and you must know how to be present without any personal agenda.

Anyone can be present with an agenda—a self-centered motive—but it takes a very conscious and inwardly free person to be present without one. Only then can you be truly open and available to the untapped creative potential existing in each moment. Only from a place of clear, loving presence can you build, create, and nurture a conscious team or organization.

The philosopher-sage, Nagarjuna, who lived in India about five hundred years after the Buddha, understood how critical enlightenment was in the art of leadership. He went so far as to say: "If a ruler cannot implement a politics of enlightenment, then he or she must abandon the throne to pursue enlightenment first."

This does not need to be taken literally. It does not mean if you are trying to foster an enlightened and harmonious work environment, you need to resign your position or office and go off on a long spiritual retreat in a mountaintop monastery somewhere. But it does mean you must take time out from your busy schedule to do some inner work.

Make awakening, your own inner peace and clarity, *the* priority in your life. Draw upon the resources which will feed your soul, nourish your heart, and illuminate your mind. Read the books, take the trainings, and get the coaching or private work to support you in this process, allowing you to return to your leadership responsibilities with renewed clarity, vision, and passion.

Above all, spend time in meditation and contemplation. As you continue to work with the practice and study the teachings I have presented in this book, take your own inner counsel. Listen not to the voices in your head, the voices telling stories of fear and worry, but to the voice of truth resonating deep within your heart and soul. Heed that voice.

Realize you are not your ever-changing stories, and not your thoughts, but rather the luminous awareness, the boundless, ever-present consciousness which is the source of your moment-by-moment experience.

The more you embody this realization, the more you will naturally empower others to live it themselves. You will model conscious, awakened behavior for them. You will inspire them to dive more deeply within themselves. You will help them discover that for those who have eyes to see, every moment is new and rich in creative possibility.

This is how you become a great leader. This is how you become a great person—great in the sense of being a true master of your own mind and emotions, a genuinely self-realized human being.

This is how the world gets transformed: each of us discovering the greatness within us, the truth of consciousness and freedom, and then sharing that truth and light with others.

How You Know When You Are Free

A woman came up to me after a lecture and asked me this: "How will I know when I am free?"

I said: "When you just don't take yourself to be anybody anymore. When you no longer hold onto any concept, story, or image of who you are. When you look inside yourself, there's no conflict, no darkness, no edges, no more tension, no fear. There's just this ever-fresh, ever-new clarity, spaciousness, ease—an inner stillness that is dynamic, vibrant, and alive. This is how you know you are free."

"And will that freedom be permanent?" she asked.

"Basically, yes. When realization happens, you know the truth of who and what you are, beyond all the beliefs and stories previously giving you your identity. And, once you know, you know. Like knowing your name, or where you live, you don't forget. Even when your body is tired, hurting, or sick, *you* always feel okay inside. Your fundamental peace and well-being remain untouched. And this is true whether you're waking, sleeping, or dreaming."

"You're always happy, then?"

"Not necessarily. If you just suffered a substantial loss—

maybe someone you love died, or you just lost your life savings in a stock market crash, or an investment gone bad—you are not going to be happy. But you will always be at peace. Nothing, not even a great loss, has the power to disturb your deep inner peace and equanimity anymore, other than momentarily."

Her eyes widened, and her face took on a dreamy, faraway look. "It sounds truly wonderful."

"It's just about being very present," I said, as I reached out and touched her hand, bringing her back to the now. "It's not about wonderful states in another dimension. It's not about being somewhere else. You know you're free when you realize there is *only* the present, this moment now, and you're always one with it. You're always at peace with this moment now. You, as an expression of consciousness, are juiced, turned on, by the unfolding of creation in this moment now."

She took a deep breath, started to relax, but then frowned. "What about ambition, hopes, dreams, the desire to do something with your life?" Suddenly, her voice rose again. "What happens to all of that?"

"Desire is still there, you're just no longer attached to it. You still have likes and dislikes, preferences, but they don't run you anymore. For example, if a desire arises to make love to your partner, and then it doesn't happen because he or she says no, there's no sense of frustration or disappointment. Or if there is, it is fleeting, and it falls away naturally. You're always in the moment, and there's always something new and interesting happening in every moment."

"What about ambition, having a sense of mission or purpose in life?"

"Ambition is there too, it's just no longer so personal, it no longer comes from the ego. As pure consciousness, you realize you are inhabiting this body, mind, and personality in order to do something. Once you find the freedom that is your true nature, what you are here to do—your personal mission, or destiny—becomes very clear. Startlingly so. Then you set about doing it. The beauty is you're no longer worried about success or failure. The joy truly is in the journey."

"And dreams at night? Do you still have them?"

"You'll still dream at night," I said, "because that's just what the brain/mind does when the body is sleeping. Dreams are a way of discharging energy, of dealing with all the images and sensory input of the day. However, with awakening, just as during the day you no longer identify with the dreams and stories inside your head, with thoughts of 'I' and 'me,' there will be no identification at night when you are sleeping, either.

"Dreams will happen. You will enjoy the show. You may even get some useful or prophetic information, but you will not personally be caught up in the dream. Just as you are free of suffering during the day, so will you be free of bad dreams at night."

Our conversation took a different direction when she asked if a person who has realized his or her true nature ever has doubts. I explained that no matter how awake we are, since we're still human, there will be moments when we are dealing with stressful or challenging circumstances, where old ego patterns involving emotional reactivity may briefly flare up.

These are the "residues" Jean Klein spoke of. I mentioned earlier that Nisargadatta Maharaj occasionally had mental or emotional reactions, or residues. If such reactions happened to Nisargadatta, who embodied the truth of liberation as powerfully as anyone, then you can be sure they are going to happen to you and me.

Something definitely shifts once you have seen with total clarity that you are *not* your story. You no longer take yourself to be the person called "Mary Smith" or "Bill Jones," but instead now know yourself as the pure, shining consciousness *expressing* as "Mary Smith" or "Bill Jones." The shift feels like passing through a final doorway, a point of no-return, where you no longer identify with the personal.

As the years go by, whenever these residues or echoes from the past do appear, they are increasingly milder and less frequent. Consciousness is like the ocean. The echoes and residues are like waves or eddies which cause a passing disturbance, but don't affect the overall clarity and stillness of the ocean.

You notice the challenging problem or difficult circumstance and gently remind yourself: "This is not who I am." You become present and remember you are not your story, but rather you are the timeless, ever-present awareness which looks at the story and experiences the emotion surrounding the story.

Calmness and tranquility then soon return. This allows you to deal with whatever problem you are facing from a practical, creative, and focused place. Indeed, all you have to do is be fully present with the problem, attuned to what it is trying to tell you, and sooner or later it will reveal its own perfect solution.

As your awakening deepens and matures, you eventually come to the place where you don't even have to remind yourself. You live constantly in the knowing of who you are. You will realize, beyond a shadow of doubt, that you are, in your essence, the same, beautiful, conscious person that you took your "teacher," or guide, to be. No longer will you place anyone on a pedestal, nor will you see them as lower, or less-than, you.

In the meantime, the point to remember is that whenever there is conflict, it is because there is, inside you, this idea of being a "person" in conflict. After all, you say to yourself, "*I* am worried, *I* am upset, *I* am unhappy." Let go of the attachment to being "somebody," to naming and labeling every experience, and you'll be free. You'll be free to share who and what you are with others as you take the action steps needed to fulfill your destiny here.

You will share the gift of freedom with others by just being who you are, whether or not you formally become a teacher of awakening. Your unconditional way of relating will give others permission to be free, whether they are consciously aware of it or not. Gone are the judgments, projections, agendas, and expectations which used to get in the way of your relating to others. They cannot help but feel this change in you, and will be changed because of it.

Awakening to freedom, as I have made clear, is a distinct event in time. It happens when you finally see that everything between your ears—the whole world of thought, belief, of "me, myself, and my story"—comes and goes, yet *you*, as awareness, the witnessing presence, are always here.

However, the embodiment of awakening, the deepening and maturing of it, is an ongoing, life-long process. This is true of every one of us. Why do I say this? Because awakening or enlightenment is, above all, *seeing* the oneness of humanity, and it is the seeing and feeling which give rise to our love of people.

It takes time to see and experience the one source, the pure consciousness, behind every pair of human eyes, particularly when people are motivated by fear, greed, and hate.

Facing Life's Challenges

There was a period of several years after I awakened when, occasionally, fear would come up, invariably around money and material survival. When these residues from the past surfaced, I would get caught up in them for a while, thinking that maybe I was "losing" my awakening. But then I would remember my true nature, relax into the knowing of it, and soon be clear and present again.

Basically, my life since that spring of 1995 has been a smooth, harmonious flow. This is what happens when you wake up: you are mostly always in the flow, and it always feels good. There is little emotional reactivity because you are not holding onto any personal story which could trigger a reaction. You truly are identified with *being*, with the consciousness which is your true nature. You feel deeply humbled, and immensely grateful.

When the daily problems and challenges of life arise, as inevitably they do, you just face them from a clear, grounded, open, and present space. Consider, for example, what happened to me with the strokes I had, which I spoke of in the beginning of the Introduction.

When I was in the emergency room at UCSF Hospital, just after the third stroke had occurred, a radiologist came by my gurney and said he wanted me to sign a waiver so he could do an angiogram. This was a procedure where they place a catheter in the groin and go up through the carotid artery, and then inject a dye into the cerebral arteries. If he then found an area of constriction, he said, he would insert a stent to open the artery back up. However, there was a twenty-five percent risk factor of my having a major stroke or dying, which was why he wanted me to sign.

These didn't sound like very good odds to me at all! It was then that I experienced a brief but strong contraction of fear, an instinctual survival response, I later realized. But since my life was on the line anyway, I signed, and then breathed and relaxed as much as possible. I came back to my normal way of being, of flowing with what was happening, one moment at a time. As it turned out, the radiologist made no intervention. I had several constricted areas in my arteries, but they were too deep to do anything about.

I remember lying in bed soon after coming home from the hospital, still in a state of extreme weakness and exhaustion, and thinking: "Thank God I'm free." If I was going to have another stroke, or even if I was going to die (and, at that point, both seemed in the realm of possibility) I was ready. Then, as the days passed and I regained a little strength, I realized I needed to make a decision: if I wanted to live, I needed to make a conscious choice to do so.

I was only fifty-seven. I had already spent four years working on a new book, an earlier version of this one. I wanted to finish it. I wanted to teach again, to share the good news, the benefits to ourselves individually and to humanity as a whole, of awakening to freedom.

So, I formed a clear intention to get well. Daily, I used the power of visualization to create more blood flow in the corollary arteries beginning to develop in the left side of my brain since the strokes. Over the next six months I had occupational and speech therapy to assist with my rehabilitation. The whole process took almost two years, but I have recovered to the point where everything, except the function of my right hand, and a slight, occasional limp in my right leg, has pretty much returned to normal. My right hand was dominant and is still paralyzed to the degree where I can't use it very well, other than to shake hands, open doors, and pick up grocery bags.

The third stroke literally knocked me on my ass. My ego was still at times identified with a "story" about being enlightened, and it was as if I had been whacked on the side of my head with a cosmic two-by-four. As a result, I now have a much more relaxed way of being and am free of any story, even about being "free."

The strokes taught me several lessons, and reinforced things I already knew. The lesson of gratitude was brought home to me. I was grateful for the friends who supported me with their love and energy, and gave me money when I really needed it.

I am also grateful that the strokes forced me to transition out of a career I wasn't passionate about (but was at peace with) into work which really is an authentic expression of me: writing about and teaching people how to be free, how to find the inner peace that does not depend upon outer circumstances.

Another lesson is the reaffirmation that life is always changing. One of the secrets of awakening is not to resist the changes, but to flow with them. In my case, I was fit and healthy at the time of my first stroke. I jogged for exercise, worked out at the gym, and had practiced yoga for over thirty years. The strokes came with no warning signs. However, I was taking the drug Vioxx for arthritis in my hands at the time of the first stroke, and maybe that was the culprit. Vioxx was soon withdrawn for the market because it was found to double the risk of heart attacks and strokes.

Anyway, I had to deal with the changes that took place in my life and learn to appreciate the gift in each new experience. This is the real meaning of the strokes and of my life now, I feel: supreme gratitude for still being here, for still being able to share my wisdom and love with others.

A Practice For Manifestation

This is a good practice to do first thing in the morning. You can even make it your meditation. Close your eyes, or keep them open. Become one with that expanded sense of pure consciousness, of radiant presence. Notice the thoughts which come and go. Do not identify with them, not even the "I" or "me" thought. Let your identity come from being *itself. You are one with the beauty, harmony, and flow of this moment now.*

Then consciously use the power of your mind to think about something you really want to create or manifest. Pull your energy in, like a magnet, and bring all the power of your presence to your manifestation. It could be anything: to create your ideal relationship, to make a certain amount of money, to find the perfect job, to build your business in some way, to exercise or improve your health, to fulfill some creative urge, to plan something new, and so on.

Get very clear about your intention, and visualize it happening. Feel it as if it has already *happened. Do an affirmation around it, if you wish, such as: "I now easily and effortlessly manifest more customers, or clients." See yourself conversing with the customers or clients, or the money coming in, or the plan taking effect. See it in your mind as already so.*

When the visualization is very clear in your mind's eye, and you can feel it in your body as if it were already so, then let it go, using an affirmation like: "And so it is…" Such a statement, uttered with your whole being, helps take any residue of "you," your ego, out of the picture. It really is about surrender, and allowing divine grace, or whatever you want to call the mysterious creative power of the universe, to have its way.

Then come back to simply being very aware and relaxed in the present. As you get up to go about your day, be aware of any action you need to take to manifest your intention into reality. Be proactive. Throughout the day, occasionally think of your intentions as a way of reminding yourself to stay focused. Otherwise, just be very present with whatever is happening and unfolding in this moment now.

Afterword

There is a Native American story I heard many years ago. It is about a young brave who is having bad dreams at night. In the dreams he owns two dogs, a white dog named Love, and a black dog named Fear. Every time he went out to feed them, the black dog snarled viciously and started attacking the white dog, such that the dreams turned into nightmares.

Desperate, he goes to the medicine man, the wisest man in the village. "The black dog keeps getting bigger and more ferocious. I'm afraid if he kills the white dog it means love is going to die in my heart, and I will lose my courage as a warrior. What should I do?"

The medicine man thought for a moment. "It's simple," he said.

"What?" the brave pleaded.

"Just feed the white dog."

Feed the white dog. Focus on love, not on fear. Stop giving energy to the dark, fearful thoughts inside your head and feed only what is positive and true, what makes you feel inwardly confident and whole.

The lesson of this charming story is good to remember when you are struggling with issues of self-doubt, personal conflict, fear, or suffering. Just like the religious stories we were told when we were young, whether Christian, Jewish, Buddhist, Hindu, Islamic, or some other tradition, this story has the power to shift our state of consciousness and give us a sense of peace and wholeness, if we let it.

But a story is still a story, no matter how charming, beautiful, or true it is. So long as our inner peace and well-being is dependent upon a story, it will always be conditional. When we no longer believe the story or the story just doesn't do it for us anymore, we are once again plunged into self-doubt and conflict.

In the book you have just read, I have presented a radically different approach to transformation, one promising to deliver you through the door to true freedom. I have described again and again the remarkably simple practice, the essence of which is learning to face your inner conflicts, self-doubt, and fears without any story whatsoever. Here are the three steps, one more time:

Step 1—Be Present With Your Experience

As you have learned by now, resistance to what is happening is the cause of personal suffering. When facing any inner conflict, struggle, or upset, that is your signal to become very present, very alert, and open to what is. Ask yourself: "What is my experience right now?" Better yet, you can even welcome the upset. After all, it is showing you where you are still not free.

Step 2—Notice The Story

Behind every reactive emotion, whether it is self-doubt, guilt, anger, envy, loneliness, anxiety, or depression, there is always a story, belief, or thought. Notice the story you are telling yourself. If it helps, you can affirm: "Uh-oh, I'm getting caught up in a story again..."

Step 3—See The Truth

Then see the truth. Observe how the thoughts, beliefs, and stories, just like the feelings and sensations, are ever changing, appearing and disappearing, but you *are the awareness which is* always *present, always here. So, be the clear, unchanging awareness you are …*

When you do this practice enough, at some level you eventually realize that what you are is simply clear, radiant, present-time awareness itself. You are the luminous, unchanging consciousness manifesting in this body, mind, and personality called "you." As this realization deepens, it will impart a new sense of meaning, purpose, and power. When you are no longer so identified with the contents of your mind—with thoughts, beliefs, and stories—you are freer of emotional stress and reactivity, and you experience more ease and harmony.

However, in order to pass through the final door to awakening or inner freedom, you have to use this practice to face *everything* in yourself, including all your demons. You have to face fear itself. To use the metaphor in the story above, you have to confront the black dog. You have to look it in the eyes and discover for yourself just how real or unreal it is.

If you truly face it and stay with it long enough, you'll discover it *isn't* real. Nothing in your mind or in your dreams is real. Only consciousness or awareness is real. Only what is timeless, changeless, and always *here* is real.

Yes, you have thoughts, including the "I" and "me" thoughts. You have a personal history. You have concepts, beliefs, ideas about your life and what you want to do, what you want to achieve or accomplish. You have memories and stories about your life. You have sensations in your body. You have feelings and emotions. You have experiences. Events and circumstances come and go in your life.

But because they are always changing, none of these *manifestations* of consciousness can possibly be who and what you are. Who and what you are is the consciousness, the radiant presence which is aware of all these ever-changing phenomena. You are the entire ocean, the boundless awareness expressing in and through this unique mind/body/person appearing as "you."

Realize the liberating truth of this notion, and you will be free; free of the attachment to and identification with the personal pronouns "I" and "me." Letting go of this identification, which is the "fourth" step, marks the final shift into freedom. You will be fully awake to your true nature. You will know yourself *as* consciousness, as an expression of the divine, the one Reality behind creation.

You will clearly see beyond all doubt the "person" you always considered yourself to be doesn't exist. It never did. It was only an idea or story in your mind that you had bought into, "believed," for a lifetime. Then you will be truly present—naturally, easily, effortlessly.

After awakening you will find your identity not in stories, not in thoughts or beliefs, not in emotions or feelings, and not in events and circumstances, but in *being* itself, in the beauty, harmony, and fullness of existence. You will still have an identity, a story in the world, as a business or professional person, as a laborer or mechanic, as an artist or musician, or as a mother or father. But now you will know, beyond a shadow of a doubt, that who and what you really are is much, much more than this.

The mind, with all of its thoughts, will no longer be a distraction. Instead, it will be a true ally, a magnificent tool for solving problems, communicating with others, and setting intentions around what you want to create. Your purpose will become clear. Love, gratitude, and affection will guide you in every aspect of your life.

This is the message in this book. This is the realization awaiting you.

Acknowledgements

Heartfelt gratitude to Gaiakai Harris, Kari Taber, Frederic Ernst, Christine Case, Cameron Pazirandeh, and Shari Faerman for their editorial feedback, and to Joe Kinnee for the great title.

Special thanks to Shelley Warren who graciously and painstakingly went through the manuscript twice, paragraph by paragraph, and suggested better ways of wording them. Thanks to Doris Davis for the final copy edit.

I also want to thank my friends from Sonoma county who helped me keep all this real: Karl and Satri Andersen, Eduardo Barr, Steve Brum, Larry Elsener, Frederic Ernst, Richard Koobatian, Richard Murphy, Sheldon Murphy, Phil Salyer and Julia Melody, and Glenn Siegel.

Much gratitude to Mary Criquet, who helped care for me when I was dealing with the most acute phase of stroke recovery. Thanks to Suzanne Taylor, who introduced me to her spiritual community in Los Angeles, and graciously hosted my gatherings in her home for more than ten years.

Many thanks, too, to my clients, students, and workshop participants. You are the reason why I am still here. Special thanks to Lee Chiacos, who assists me and leads the morning meditation and chi gong at my Esalen workshops, and to John Smith, who attended in 2008 and gave me honest feedback on the practice which helped refine it to what it is now.

Thanks to John Raatz and the Visioneering Group who recommended a new cover design, steered me to the designer, Ben Cziller (who did an amazing job), and gave invaluable input during the process.

Lastly, many thanks to Emile Trienekens of the Netherlands, who invested in the initial hardcover printing.

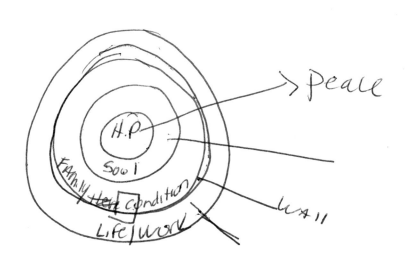

Peace

H.P.

Soul

Family Hea Condition

Life/Work

Wall